RENO HIGH SCHOOL L

W9-CQC-825

331.702 Roesch, Roberta Fle
Ro
         Money, jobs and
         futures   532

DATE DUE			

ESEA PURCHASE
WASHOE COUNTY SCHOOL DISTRICT
RENO, NEVADA

RENO HIGH SCHOOL LIBRARY.
532

MONEY, JOBS AND FUTURES

MONEY, JOBS and FUTURES

A Guide for Young People on the Move

ROBERTA ROESCH

Macrae Smith Company

PHILADELPHIA

COPYRIGHT © 1965 BY ROBERTA ROESCH

All rights reserved. No part of this book may be reproduced in any form without permission in writing from the publisher, except by a reviewer, who may quote brief passages in a review to be printed in a magazine or newspaper.

Library of Congress Catalog Card Number 65-16331
MANUFACTURED IN THE UNITED STATES OF AMERICA

6508

Second Printing

ACKNOWLEDGMENTS

The author acknowledges with much appreciation the assistance given her by the many, many people and organizations who contributed background material used in the research and writing of this book. Although it is impossible to acknowledge every person and organization she has consulted, the following have been particularly helpful. Grateful thanks are due to all:

Allstate Insurance Company; American Hospital Association; The American Legion; American Music Conference; American National Red Cross; Lydia Bickford, Gilbert Youth Service; Boy Scouts of America; Chamber of Commerce of the United States; Cleanliness Bureau, The Soap and Detergent Association; Corning Glass Works Foundation; Council for Professional Education for Business; Distributive Education Clubs of America; Empire Crafts Corporation; Famous Artists Schools; Famous Photographers Schools; Dr. Mortimer R. Feinberg, Baruch School, City College of New York; Future Homemakers of America; Girl Scouts of the United States of America; International Business Machines Corporation; Interboard Committee on Christian Vocations, The Methodist Church; Institute of Life Insurance; Institute of Student Opinion; Kiwanis International; Metropolitan Life Insurance Company; The National Association of State Supervisors of Distributive Education; National Child Labor Committee; The National Committee on Employment of Youth; National Consumer Finance Association; National Education Association of the United States; National 4-H Service Committee, Inc.; National Home Study Council; The National Thrift Committee, Inc.; The National Vocational Guidance Association; New York State Employment Service; The Public Affairs Committee; The Salvation Army; State of Illinois Board of Vocational Education; The Taconic Foundation, Inc.; United Church of Christ Publications; U. S. Department of Commerce; U. S. Department of Health, Education and Welfare; U. S. Department of Labor, Bureau of Labor Statistics; United States National Student Association; State University of New York (Bureau of Guidance, Bureau of Trade and Technical Education, Vocational Education Research Department, Vocational Instructional Services), Walt Disney Productions; Westinghouse Electric Corporation; Young & Rubicam, Research Department; Young Presidents' Organization, Inc.; Young Men's Christian Association.

In addition to the organizations listed above the author wishes to thank the following organizations for permission to include quotations from copyrighted material: The American National Red Cross for permission to reprint suggestions from Frank W. Erwin, deputy director of selection for the Peace Corps from *The American Red Cross Journal;* Enterprise Publications for permission to quote from its booklet *Adjusting To Change;* National Council of the Young Men's Christian Association for permission to reprint summer job letter from *National HI-Y Ways,* May 1964; Public Affairs Committee for permission to quote from their pamphlet *Worrying About College?* by Fred M. Hechinger; Scholastic Magazines for permission to reprint material from their study of the youth market covering the income and savings of a cross section of young people from 7th through 12th grade; Science Research Associates for permission to reprint a rundown of high school courses from "My Educational Plans" by Harold L. Munson; University of Rochester for permission to quote from its Service Bulletin, *Hints On Vacation College Prospecting.*

CONTENTS

AUTHOR'S NOTE

My aim in writing this book has been to present, through fun and fact, the wonderful story of growing up!

As young Americans you're growing up in a turning point in history. A whole new world is ahead of you. But this whole is made up of many parts, as you'll find out in the following chapters. And it takes work—plus hopes and dreams—to shape the whole that's your future!

A book is also a whole that's made up of many parts, and many people have had a part in the whole that is now this book. I've listed their names within the text or at the front of the book.

But no kind of "thank you" would be complete without a special "thank you" to my husband, Philip Roesch, and my children, Jeffrey, Bonnie, and Merry—who make my own life a whole; my secretary, Dagny Jensen, who helped in the research and typing; my editors at King Features Syndicate, who have opened so many doors; the readers of my daily column, who share so much of themselves with me; the young people all over the country who have asked and answered questions, with special thanks especially due to the students and staff in the Wood County schools in Parkersburg, West Virginia, and the Westwood, New Jersey, Junior and Senior High Schools; the employers and personnel directors who gave this book so much time and thought, with special thanks again being due to Champion Papers, Inc., the Borden Company, the Grand Union Company, the Dow Chemical Company, Hess's Department Store, Four Star Television, Lake House Hotel, Tip Top Dairies, Burroughs Corporation and the Hoover Company.

I'm grateful to each one!

ROBERTA ROESCH

Westwood, New Jersey

MONEY, JOBS AND FUTURES

1

Raise the Curtain and
See Yourself

THE subject of this book is *you,* and its purpose is the building of your future—with emphasis on part-time jobs, summer jobs, business services, paying hobbies, a good personality, education, and all the many other things that prepare you to make a good living and bring you success.

Today, as one of the more than twenty-two million teens in our population (with millions more to come in this decade) you're writing your ticket to your future in a world that's challenged by the widest horizons and tallest heights any generation of teens has ever faced.

But an age of wonders is your future, too, and your opportunities will be what you make them, whether you envision for yourself the role of banker or baker, teacher or technician, scientist or stenographer, philosopher or plumber. As President Lyndon B. Johnson said in speaking to your generation, "You have been born to man's most exceptional opportunity. You are challenged to work toward the great and the grand."

It isn't always easy, though, when childhood is behind you and adulthood is ahead, to know how to reach your own most exceptional opportunity and what to plan vocationally for the great and the grand.

But, in your own words, and from all parts of the country, young people have framed their questions and problems to their advisors this way:

About Your Abilities

Is a person's best ability always synonomous with the subject he likes best or in which he gets the best marks?

How can I be certain that I know myself?

Am I really talented in the things in which I think I'm talented?

About Your Education

How hard will it be for me to get further education?

Will I be accepted in a college?

How will I find out about entrance requirements and the right courses to take?

What happens if I don't go to college?

How will I get money for college?

Is there any way to alleviate this awful "getting-into-college" stress that I'm living through?

How will I pick a good school and know it's the right school for me?"

About Your Job and Future

What's the right way to plan for a future job?

How do I know what I'd like to do best and what I'd be best suited for?

In what work will I be happy and still make enough money to support myself and a family?

What are the most important things to consider in deciding on my future?

About Part-Time Jobs and Earning Money Now

Where can a fourteen-year-old get a job?

What's the best way to get a job?

How do you apply for summer jobs and what summer jobs are in demand?

What's available in part-time or after-school jobs?

Do part-time jobs help or hinder a teenager's experiences?

Where do you get the "in" to summer jobs?

How do you get started on a money-making hobby or part-time business of your own?

What are the advantages of a business of your own or a hobby that pays?

About Personality and Popularity

How can I get along with people and be accepted by them?

Why can't I open my mouth without putting my foot in it and accidentally offending someone?

Why am I either too shy or too flippant? I never feel I have the proper attitude, especially in front of teachers.

Is there any way to be more patient, mature and tactful?

Will I always have to go through life being so unsure of myself?

The answers to these questions are the chapters of this book. And the aim of this book is to show you how to get the right start to your right future by picturing for you how other people do it and how you can do it yourself.

Knowing these things is important for girls as well as boys, since a good many girls now growing up will be earning their own living for a good many years in the future.

Actually, women now outnumber men by two and one-half million, so not all girls who are planning their futures will carry those traditional orange blossoms. Some will fulfill a dual role, with a husband and family plus a job. Many girls will marry at an early age, have their children at an equally early age and be ready to return to the job world, either because they have to or because they want to, when their children enter school.

In fact, nine girls out of ten will be busy making a living at some time in the future, since women workers are increasing at nearly twice the rate of men. Also, according to authorities in the United States Labor Department, one out of every three workers is a woman, while three out of five are married.

Consequently, for either a boy or girl, the two vital questions are: To make a living and build a good life for myself (1) what shall I do? and (2) how shall I do it? Certainly it's normal to be uncertain about these things in one's teens, but this is the right time to start taking stock of yourself, since the sooner a young person discovers where he fits the framework of jobs and vocations the sooner he can start building a successful future.

Can there be a timetable for selecting jobs and futures? Many teenagers ask, "Is it better to decide who you are and what you want to be once and for all, and then stick to it, or is it better to try a variety of different things till you find the right work?"

Unfortunately, there's no one answer that's always right. The answer varies according to people. Some find themselves very early. Others flounder and let years slip by. In the final analysis, if a person spends his life in a job that gives him his own definition of success, it doesn't matter whether that job decision came on the first, second, or thirty-fifth try. Nevertheless, it's right to start looking for ways to discover oneself as early as possible. When a person knows who he is and what he wants to do, he suddenly has purpose and direction. His days in school take on meaning because he knows where he'd like school to take him.

One girl who illustrates the great adventure of discovering one's own abilities early in life is youthful Bernice Chang, who seems destined to be a leading scientist of the future. Her interest in science started when she was in third grade. She heard that Russia was making great scientific strides, decided then and there that she wanted to be a scientist, began building toward that aim, and, as a result, reached the top of her class by her Senior year in high school. Bernice won a Westinghouse Science Talent Search award for her study in human genetics, the field of work dealing with inherited characteristics. She intends to be a research geneticist.

Henry Ford was another person who discovered himself and started to build toward his future early in life.

At ten, for instance, young Henry made it his business to learn all he could about clocks and watches so he could earn money fixing them for people.

By the time he was twelve, he went a step further and persuaded his teacher to let him organize the building of a forge in the school playground. At fourteen he designed and built a dam across a stream—and at this point demonstrated his executive ability by persuading a group of friends to accumulate material and build the dam while he supervised!

At sixteen Ford took a part-time job as an assistant mechanic and subsequently decided that he would like to work on steam engines, or something similar, for the rest of his life.

Barney Tobey, a top cartoonist, discovered himself, not at ten, not in third grade, but during his high school years, when his success in school publications turned his mind toward cartooning as a career. But even when he received an art scholarship to help him reach that aim, Tobey couldn't afford to take the scholarship. Instead he had to go to work as an art apprentice. In this kind of job, an aspiring artist inks in letters, draws outlines, pastes up ads, runs errands, fills inkwells, sweeps floors and does other miscellaneous jobs. But, as Tobey found out, any ambitious young artist who takes this kind of job can also look over established artists' shoulders and learn as he or she works.

Consequently, while Tobey worked as an art apprentice, he learned all he could from the job and kept his eye on his ultimate goal by spending his lunch hours trying his hand at humorous magazine covers.

Ultimately, because of his industry and his long range goal, he found himself by the time that he was 19 when he sold three illustrations, all at one time, to *The New Yorker!*

Any way you look at it, the Bernice Changs, Henry Fords and Barney Tobeys who discover themselves so early in life are the exceptions rather than the rule.

But you can make a start at finding yourself now—and have fun and help while you do it—by giving yourself the "See Yourself" quizzes to be found throughout this book.

Use a notebook or pad for your answers so you can keep the results to yourself.

As you proceed to study your capabilities and think things over, you'll gradually reach a point where you'll want to discuss your aptitudes, interests, problems and potential vocations with your parents, teachers, and guidance counselors, but it's fun to start discovering yourself on your own. The first quiz will help you see how you compare, as far as teenage problems go, with other teenagers throughout the country, who have pinpointed these problems as the ones that bother them most. Run through the list to see where you stand. Then make a list of your own problems.

"SEE YOURSELF" TEENAGE PROBLEM QUIZ

1. I feel like an outsider in school and other large crowds when people don't ask me to join a group.
2. When I try out for something and don't make it, I can't get over the feeling I'm a failure.
3. Even though I've tried, I can't find enough ways to earn money for my clothes and school expenses.
4. Good grades are very important to me, so I worry about getting them and maintaining them.
5. It's hard for me to talk to people.
6. When people do things better than I do I brood about it at home and act sullen and irritable.
7. I can't always get along with my family and other people.
8. I'm afraid to try things for fear people will laugh if I'm no good at them.
9. If I do a bad job when I know I can do better I can't stop worrying about it.
10. I'm not as popular as I'd like to be.
11. I don't know what career to choose.
12. Finding a way to get money for college and worrying

about whether I'll be accepted are my two greatest problems.

13. When I hear my parents say, "Just wait till you have to make your own living," I wonder how well I'll do a job.

14. I'm afraid to speak up and say what I think for fear I might be wrong.

15. I'm a sorehead and get mad too much.

16. I get discouraged easily and give up on things before I really try because I'm not as good at doing things as other people.

17. I'm not good-looking and no one ever looks at me twice.

18. I don't like myself when I know I've done something wrong.

19. Im unhappy when I miss out on functions that other people my age attend.

20. I'm not sure what I want to be in life. I really haven't a goal.

21. I'd like to have a bigger voice in things that go on around me.

22. I spend more time in trying to get organized than in getting things done.

23. I can't save money.

24. My biggest problem is making friends. I've never had a very close friend.

25. It bothers me when I can't convince people that I'm not still a kid.

Regardless of the problems you have had to check, you're not alone with any of them. And you can get help in solving them, too, not only from the chapters in this book but also from your parents, teachers, guidance counselors and other people in whom you have confidence.

If, in addition to this kind of help, you still need extra help to discover yourself vocationally, you can always enlist the help of a vocational counselor, who will talk with you and give you vocational and aptitude tests that will spot your abilities and possibilities more precisely than you can do it yourself.

Despite all the help you seek from outsiders, though, you'll have to have confidence in your own decisions and —in the end—decide for yourself who you are and what you can be.

One way for a person to get views of what he thinks he'd like to be is to indulge in the solo act of constructive daydreaming. When done with a purpose, spending some time alone in daydreaming is a wonderful way to get to know, understand, and like yourself.

This liking oneself is important. "A person who does not approve of himself cannot be happy," says Lucille Ball, an actress much admired by young people. "Self-love is a very necessary ingredient.

"At first encounter, that statement may seem shocking. We are accustomed to thinking of self-love as a negative, if not odious, quality. We don't like conceited people. It is a vice to be self-centered.

"But the self-love we are talking about is none of these. Self-love is simply having a little charity towards yourself and understanding that you, too, are just another struggling human. It means not making undue demands upon yourself. In short, give yourself a break. Bertrand Russell once remarked, 'A man who is not at peace with himself cannot be at peace with his fellows.' The Bible tells us, 'Thou shalt love thy neighbor as thyself.'

"In other words, the Bible presupposes that we love ourselves. Self-love is implied as the standard."

This preoccupation with yourself and your thoughts can sometimes make parents forget you're young when they tell you to stop "just sitting there while there's a bed to be made or garbage to go out!"

But from a broader point of view they know also that dreamtime is another word for teen-time—so daydreams become you very well when you use your daydreaming hours to mull over real-life challenges and how you'll meet them.

Daydreaming doesn't become you, though, if you use it as an entrance to an imaginative fantasyland where you see yourself in a dream world instead of in a world of real people and action. This kind of dreaming gets you nowhere fast, so shove it out of your life and take your cue instead from Rudyard Kipling's lines:

> *If you can dream—and not make dreams*
> *   your master . . .*
> *If you can fill the unforgiving minute*
> *With sixty seconds' worth of distance run,*
> *Yours is the Earth and everything that's*
> *   in it,*
> *And—which is more—you'll*
> *   be a Man, my son!*

(P.S. You'll also be a Woman!)

As you daydream, start picturing in your mind and on paper your future image, too, because—almost always—when you know where you want to go and how you're going to get there your chances of getting there will be better. Also, when you have a clear image of what you want to do you can draw up a plan of action to make your education, hobbies and early jobs direct steps for getting there.

It doesn't matter, as we said before, whether your image of yourself is cast as a banker or baker, teacher or technician, scientist or stenographer, philosopher or plumber, as long as it's right for you. But it is important that your career image provide you with more than just a way to earn a living. It should show promise of letting you live your life to the best of your abilities. It should promise you satisfaction and enjoyment and make you feel you'll be achieving a useful purpose in your life.

To make sure your future image is adequate for your needs, you can write in your "See Yourself" notebook a description of yourself as you'd like to be ten years from now.

One girl who wants to be a teacher wrote:

"Ten years from today I hope to be a happy, successful person.

"First of all, I hope to be teaching French in a high school, since teaching is to be one-half of my life's goal.

"To complete my goal I hope to have a home and family at some future date, too. At the present time I haven't set any particular time for that, except for the fact that it will definitely be after college.

"I hope ten years in the future will hold for me my present goal. I plan to reach that goal, too."

Actually, this young girl has written down a pretty good starter blueprint for her future.

In fact, she has blueprinted a lot more detail than two ambitious high school boys questioned, who need to etch a few more details on their sketches of the future.

The first declared, "Ten years from now I hope to be a leader in my profession."

The second said, "Ten years from now I hope to be in an office dictating letters to an attractive secretary while a man paints 'President' on my office door."

In looking ahead you'll stand a much greater chance of "making it" by trying to be a little more specific about the general field you hope to be in and by having at least a few definite plans for getting there.

At this point you don't have to freeze on one specific job in one field without investigating the opportunities in several fields through the best vocational tryouts of all—summer jobs, part-time jobs, special services, hobbies, and volunteer work. But you should start viewing job fields now and applying them to your interests, even if you have to do more selecting and reselecting later on.

For all the people who discover themselves and their job aims early there are just as many others, like Ben Maddow, who ultimately built himself a threefold career in Hollywood—but only after many years of trying various jobs.

Maddow started out as a pre-med student. Then he switched to biophysics. Still later, he did graduate work in mathematics. In between, he wrote poetry.

In spite of all this educational background, Maddow's first job was pushing a garment truck for twenty-five dollars a month. After that, he worked in a restaurant for two years. Next, he switched to selling. Later, he worked in a hospital as a laboratory assistant.

In World War II, Maddow entered the Army and was ultimately assigned to an Air Corps motion picture unit, which gradually pointed the way to a delayed career in motion pictures.

Subsequently, at the urging of friends, he tried his hand at writing for motion pictures—and succeeded! Still later, by tying all the varied threads of his varied background together, Maddow found himself in the right job field and became a successful motion picture writer-director-producer.

Not every story of floundering has such a happy ending, of course, and that's why it's a good idea to see yourself now as you'd like to be in ten years.

Once you devise your "image," follow it with three lists.

In the first list write down everything you'll need to change or improve about yourself to put the image you've conceived into effect. In the second list, outline a general plan, as you see it now, of all you'll have to do to make this image come to life. In the third list specify all the things about your life you'll have to change to produce the person you want to be.

As you read through the rest of this book you'll make changes and additions to the lists you're making. But starting to make lists now will give you something to start with as well as something to live up to.

You are the most important element in this book, regardless of who you are and what you've done in the past! There is not a person reading it without some potential for the future.

Ralph Waldo Emerson said, "Each man is one more lump of clay to hold the world together." In your language, this means there's a job for you ahead, and the best way to find it is to develop your best abilities as much as you can.

Actually, most people can do many things well enough to make a living at them, so it doesn't matter what you do as long as it's right for you and as long as you learn to excel at it. Dr. John W. Gardner, President of the Carnegie Foundation, once said, "An excellent plumber is infinitely more admirable than an incompetent philosopher."

With this in mind, it's time to move on to the highly exciting adventure of discovering who you are and where you are going.

2

Test Yourself

Now that you have written down in black and white an image of what you'd like to be, you're ready for more of the tests.

You'll find five more in this chapter. They include, a "Present Interest and Abilities" test, an "Achievements So Far" test, a "Strength and Weakness" test, an "Aptitude" test, and a "Personality" test.

High school students in a cross-sectional survey were asked, "Do you feel you know who you are and what you want to be in the future?" Here are some of their answers:

"I honestly don't know."

"In many ways I feel I've learned to know myself by trying to succeed in simple tasks and by trying to fulfill them to the best of my ability. When I encounter problems, I try to think out the problem myself and decide the best way to conquer the situation."

"I've learned about myself by applying my abilities to specific situations."

"I've gained a general idea of my abilities through tests

I have taken. But I still don't know what I'm going to do in the future."

"I've learned about my abilities and my goals by working at small jobs and services."

"I've figured out many things about myself through discussions with my parents and through trying to determine things on my own."

"I'm learning about myself through my everyday living."

"I'm getting to know myself through my interests."

"I'm reasonably sure of who I am and what my purpose in life is. I've arrived at this through self-evaluation and a lot of mistakes."

"I don't know who I am. But I do know a limited amount about my abilities from personal experience."

"I can't answer 'yes' or 'no' since there are so many experiences to which I haven't as yet been subjected. Because of this I can't say that I understand myself. I realize some of my abilities, of course. But there are many things I haven't had the opportunity to try."

"I've grown to know myself through various ways. I feel my friends, my attitude toward school, religion, family and grades, as well as my achievements and my failures, have helped me see myself and know myself."

"I've learned to know myself by thinking about the things I can do and want to do."

"I know myself pretty well so far. But I've never really tested my capabilities for the future."

"I've found out where I stand through my family, my social life, and my school curriculum."

"I've learned to know myself by thinking about myself."

Some of the young people have come a long way, while others are still floundering.

Here are some tests to help you measure your progress, none of them intended to be the same kind of aptitude, interest, achievement or intelligence test your school guidance department administers. Nor is any test designed to cover everything on which you'll be tested in vocational guidance tests. Each one is a "do it yourself," designed to give you a clearer view of where you stand right now.

No single test will tell all, of course. But a combination of the tests in this chapter will give you some valuable clues.

The "Present Interests and Abilities" test and the "Achievements So Far" test are starters that should be taken and evaluated together.

"SEE YOURSELF" PRESENT INTERESTS AND ABILITIES TEST

To take this first test, head one sheet of paper "Interests" and another sheet "Abilities." Under "Interests," list what you like to do. Under "Abilities," list what you can do. Write down each thought as it occurs to you. The arrangement doesn't matter at this point.

Here's how one tenth grader worked out this first test:

Present Interests

Taking piano lessons
Making my own clothes
Joining organizations in which I can work with people
Reading
Playing the piano for community and church affairs
Painting and decorating my room
Copying things from magazines to make for my room
Dancing
Attending parties
Taking part in plays

Present Abilities
Doing things with my music
Sewing
Acting
Organizing people to work together

Immediately after the "Achievements So Far" test we'll analyze together what this tenth grade girl can determine from her findings. As we do this for the girl, you'll get some idea of how to evaluate your own findings.

Before we do this, however, take the "Achievements So Far" quiz next.

"SEE YOURSELF" ACHIEVEMENTS-SO-FAR TEST

To sharpen the focus on yourself through this quiz, list your ten most important achievements so far. Some of your achievements may be big and some may be small. But everyone has accomplished something by the time he or she is in the teens, so list what you think you've done best.

This list can include achievements in school and at home, extracurricular work, hobbies, volunteer work, and jobs, to mention just a few areas in which you've probably accomplished something.

Here's the way one girl answered the "Interests and Abilities" quiz.

Achievements So Far
My A's in music
My election to several offices in the clubs I belong to
My friends
The parts I've had in school plays
My success in decorating my own room
The times I've been on the honor roll
My good relationships with my teachers and family
The clothes I've made for myself

The babysitting jobs I have
No other achievements so far.

On the whole, the list this girl has made tends to high-light music, enjoyment of people, and an artistic and crea-tive bent. These conclusions are reached, quite obviously, by running down the list and counting the number of times each item has been mentioned. You can do the same thing when you're ready to analyze your lists. It will show you whether your lists indicate a pattern of specific ten-dencies or whether they go off in so many directions you can't pinpoint any one or two special interests right now. Either result, incidentally, is normal at this stage of the game.

Whatever happens, however, initial tests like these will certainly not be conclusive enough to give you sure-fire directions to your entire future, but they indicate what you've accomplished so far and how much there is left to accomplish.

"SEE YOURSELF" STRENGTH AND WEAKNESS QUIZ

Now probe a little deeper by taking the "Strength and Weakness" test.

It will help you plot the future by spotlighting your successes and weaknesses in the past. Mark yourself "strong," "average" or "weak" in your notebook beside the number of each question.

1. Working with my hands doing mechanical things or using machines
2. Working with my head, using my reasoning power with facts and figures
3. Working with my hands doing creative things
4. Working with people
5. Working by myself
6. Developing ideas

7. Finding jobs and earning money
8. Participating in extracurricular activities
9. Taking part in sports
10. Maintaining good school grades
11. Excelling in music, art or other artistic courses
12. Excelling in science and mathematics courses
13. Excelling in English and history courses
14. Excelling in language courses

As you complete this test you'll find that very often your strengths and weaknesses and your likes and dislikes go hand in hand. This is to be expected, and is true for most people. You'll also find that many of the strengths and weaknesses and likes and dislikes you have now will follow you through most of your life—so if your weaknesses predominate, start improving now.

"SEE YOURSELF" APTITUDE TEST

No inventory would be complete without an aptitude test, so here's one for a starter. Not every aptitude is listed. This test just skims the surface, but it is fun to take, and it gives you a definite start in pinpointing some of your aptitudes. Printed beside each aptitude is a possible job field.

Check your rating in your notebook beside the right number.

Have you some of these advantages that fit you for special work?

1. Ability to handle many details at one time (purchasing)
2. Ability to work under pressure (advertising)
3. Ability to work with the sick and disabled (medical and related fields)
4. Ability to remember figures instead of names (accounting)

5. Ability to visualize things like geometric conceptions and designs (engineer, architect or draftsman)

Do you . . .

6. Like to fix meals for others? (cooking, baking and the food field)
7. Like to work out of doors? (agriculture, forestry, horticulture)
8. Like to maintain orderly records? (clerical work)
9. Enjoy helping people with problems? (professional counseling field)
10. Like conducting experiments and learning the how and why of things? (chemistry, physics and science)
11. Like serving people? (personal service fields)
12. Grasp ideas and use words well? (writer, lawyer, teacher, salesman)
13. Sing or play an instrument and enjoy long hours of practicing? (music field)
14. Appreciate color and balance and have lots of imagination? (artist, actor, designer)
15. Have deep religious convictions? (religious work, church and allied fields)

As we mentioned before, this very simple aptitude test is only an introductory one for raising the curtain on your future possibilities. To get a deeper general view, you may later want to take a widely known vocational guidance test known as the Kuder Preference Record. When the time comes, the guidance department in your school can tell you about that.

In the meantime, though, this "See Yourself" test will help you pave the way for exploring jobs and futures.

"SEE YOURSELF" PERSONALITY TEST

There's a whole chapter ahead of you on personality and popularity; but just for the fun of it, right now, take this test on the traits below.

Your ability counts in your job and future, but your personality does, too! So where you're weak, get stronger. And where you're strong, do the same. Rate yourself "weak," "potentially strong," or "strong" beside the right number in your notebook.

1. Sincerity
2. Honesty
3. Ambition
4. Patience
5. Initiative and leadership
6. Understanding and thoughtfulness
7. Kindness
8. Tact and diplomacy
9. Self-reliance
10. High moral values
11. Self-control
12. Cheerfulness
13. Neatness
14. Courtesy and good manners
15. Dependability
16. Responsibility
17. Humility
18. Willingness to cooperate at home, school or work
19. Loyalty
20. Punctuality

With this group of tests behind you, go back through each test and compare your findings. Then take your time as you think about jobs, because choosing a career or vocation has to be a thoughtful process. It shouldn't be a snap decision.

Once you have a general idea of the field of work that appeals to you, keep your eye on the "image" you devised in Chapter I. Also keep reviewing the lists of the things you'll need to do to achieve your future plans.

At the same time, have confidence in your ability to

achieve your goal. Read books, magazine articles, and newspaper stories about the job fields that interest you. And keep a special file of the information you find most helpful.

Also, at this point in the exciting adventure of planning your future, start earning some money right now with a part-time job, special service, or paying hobby.

3

Earn Money Now Through Part-Time Jobs, Special Services or Hobbies

"I know I want to do something to make money while I'm in school, but I don't know what I want to do," says one young boy interviewed on this subject.

"If I had my choice I'd like a job as a nurse's aid," a girl honor student adds.

"I'd like to work in a gas station"—this from a boy with a ready smile.

"And I'd like a job where I'd be in contact with people," announces a cross-country star who plans to be a minis-ter.

Other students around the country questioned on part-time work say they'd like to find jobs typing, selling, working with children or doing "whatever I can find."

Many of them admit, however, that even though they want to work they've never earned any money, aside from working for their parents, because too many part-time jobs seem to be for people eighteen and older.

As one boy puts it, "I've applied several times for jobs in some of the plants in my community. But every time, I've been told that the plant doesn't hire anyone under eighteen."

This can happen—usually for one of two good reasons. First, some individual organizations establish their own policy of employing no one under eighteen. Second, the law itself sometimes forbids employment of young people under eighteen when certain jobs and certain working conditions are involved.

Be that as it may, a lot of teens under eighteen are finding ways to earn money, just as they have in every generation.

Herbert Hoover, our thirty-first President, went to work as an office boy when he was fifteen in order to support himself and earn money for college.

Screen star Kirk Douglas started earning his way while still in grade school by delivering newspapers at 5 A.M., before his school day began, and finishing at 7 P.M. Even with that kind of industry, though, Douglas had to work for a year after high school graduation before he could go to college. And when he did get enough funds to start, he had to hitchhike his way to St. Lawrence University, ultimately arriving on top of a truck filled with fertilizer!

In the sixties, young people on the move are still finding opportunities to work. According to the National Consumer Finance Association, for example, recent figures show that of the 12½ million fourteen- to seventeen-year-old boys and girls enrolled in school in 1963 one in every six was employed at some time during each week. Another survey, made by *American Girl,* shows that before age thirteen fifty-seven per cent of today's girls have earned money by doing non-family chores and sixty-eight per cent have done baby sitting for other families' children.

All this proves, of course, what lots of us know—that teenagers have much to offer in the working world!

In many cases, those of you in your teens are more suited for certain jobs than older people. You're quick to learn. You're able to work for a reasonable wage. And you're loaded to the brim with that priceless commodity, energy.

Those of you now earning money earn it in many ways —though in many cases your favorite ways of earning it are by assisting teachers, typing, filing, selling, helping in gas stations, stocking shelves, packing orders and working behind counters and cash registers. Mostly, your earning projects are divided into three patterns:

Part-time jobs for which you're hired by an employer.
Your own businesses or special services.
Hobbies you turn into cash.

Let's look at ways to get into these projects.

Part-Time Jobs

In order to get a part-time job you need to do several things. To begin with, you need another session of self-analysis to see what you have to offer that someone will want to buy.

What skills have you that will fill an employer's need? Can you type, take shorthand, file or keep books? Would you be good behind a counter? Are your figure and face a combination to put you in business as a model? Are you such a help in the kitchen you're a natural for a restaurant? Once you have a skill to sell—or know how to acquire a skill—your next step is to find out how to fit that skill to the job world.

Labor Laws

Labor laws on the jobs you can hold before you reach eighteen vary slightly from state to state.

For the most part, though, you can follow the United States Department of Labor's child labor laws for part-time jobs you're likely to consider. All of these laws have been devised as safeguards against employment that might be detrimental to your health and welfare.

According to the laws, teenagers at sixteen may be employed in any occupation other than an occupation declared hazardous by the Secretary of Labor. Also at sixteen you may be employed for any number of hours and during any periods of time.

At fourteen and fifteen, however, you may not be employed during school hours. At other times you may work at certain jobs for a limited number of hours in such places as retail establishments, food service businesses and gasoline service. Specific information on laws in your state can be obtained from your local school principal or your state labor commissioner.

Job Opportunities Open to You

Job opportunities open to you in retail establishments, food service businesses and gasoline services include office and clerical work; cashiering; selling; modeling; art work; window trimming; price marking; packing; shelving; assembling orders; and making deliveries or doing errands by foot, bicycle, or public transportation.

Other jobs available to you are clean-up work; ground

maintenance; gasoline and oil dispensing; courtesy service; and car cleaning, washing, and polishing.

In food service or kitchen work, you can take jobs using dishwashers, toasters, dumb-waiters, popcorn poppers, milk shake blenders and coffee grinders. You can also clean vegetables and fruits and wrap, seal, label, weigh, process and stock goods if your work is in an area removed from outside freezers, meat coolers, or spots where meat is prepared for sale.

Your Part-Time Jobs May Lead to a Future

Once you match your skill to an employment need, you're on your way to a job—and maybe to a future!

Sandy Schippers, for example, a young girl with an exciting modeling job in an Allentown, Pennsylvania, department store, got her start for this future as a high school student when she matched her salable skill, photographing children, to a department store's need for a part-time "Santa's Helper" the Christmas before she graduated. After Christmas she continued working.

The summer after high school graduation Sandy's life took a different turn when she was chosen "Miss Bucks County Poultry Association Queen." And that title came not only because of her beauty but also because—along with working and going to school—she'd managed to grade eggs on her father's poultry breeding farm, too.

As a result of her title, plus her contact with her former employer, retail executive Max Hess, Sandy's future got its start when she was selected to be a full-time model in the store where she'd once worked part-time.

Another person who matched his skill to an employer's need and thereby got his start toward a future career was Arthur E. Taylor, now an executive in the educational toys field.

For most of Taylor's school days his ambition for the future was to work in the education field. But in order to go to school to get his own education he had to work after school and on Saturdays. Since one of his skills was book-keeping, he landed a job keeping books in a toy union office.

As a result of his first association with the toy business Taylor, an imaginative and creative person, began to devise ways for certain toys to be used as tools of learning. Consequently, since teaching jobs were hard to get in the depression years when Taylor finished college, he found a job in a toy firm, becoming a stock boy with a college degree!

With that as his start he went on to develop educational toys and ultimately rose to his present executive spot.

Working Papers

Generally speaking, you'll need working papers to work for an outside employer, even on a part-time or after-school basis. In different states they're called by different names, so you'll hear them referred to as employment certificates, work permits, age certificates, or working papers, depending on the state in which you live. You can find out how to get them by getting in touch with your local school principal or your state labor commissioner.

In order to obtain the papers, you'll need your birth certificate or baptismal record as documentary proof of your age. Chances are you'll also need a statement from your prospective employer describing the work you'll be doing.

Some states will require, in addition, (1) a statement from your doctor, (2) consent from your parents, and (3) a school record that shows the last grade you completed.

Your Own Business or Special Service

It's possible that instead of getting working papers and working for someone else your best way to earn money will be through your own business or special service.

Many young people have made glowing reports on the cash they are collecting as they baby-sit, work as household helpers or chore boys, clean out chicken coops, sell greeting cards and magazines, wash cars, care for lawns and gardens, sell home-grown flowers, make and sell articles of leather and beadwork, clean basements, wax floors, take down screens, put up storm windows, do errands for mothers tied down with small children, run toy repair services, and go from door to door painting street numbers on curbs in front of homes.

For this kind of work, again, your first step is to ask yourself what you can do particularly well. For instance, does your knitting cause a sensation? Can you clean up a yard or a basement better than anyone on the block? Are you good at minding children? Have you a talent for giving parties?

One sixteen-year-old-girl decorates oval bars of soap with flowers, pebbles, wool, paint, gilt, yarn, ribbon, decals, and cut-outs and sells them, as decorative items, from door to door.

A fifteen-year-old boy exceptionally good in shop builds birdhouses and then paints and trims them to look like the houses of people who give him orders.

Two sisters who knit while they watch television take orders for custom-made mohair sweaters. Customers provide the wool and the girls provide the labor.

Three high school basketball players who live in a good-sized suburb have a going Saturday business taking out trash and running errands. They canvassed the neighborhood for people who have money to pay for these services but no one to do the work.

To start a successful service there are certain things you need to do. Here are the most important:

Have You What It Takes?

Before you begin, ask yourself whether you're indulging in wishful thinking or whether you really want to work. Have you the quality it takes to stick with things? Have you the time? Are you willing to be at the beck and call of customers? Will you work when they want jobs done instead of when you feel like working? And can you say no to your friends when work interferes with fun?

Know Your Markets

If you don't look into possible markets and find out who will buy what you're offering or who needs your service, you may not succeed.

If you find a potential market, however—and we hope you will!—give yourself an extra chance to succeed by going to your library and asking your librarian to suggest some helpful literature on starting businesses and special services. Reading how other people do things will help you be more successful yourself. Besides reading, seek advice and opinions from older, experienced people.

Make Your Service or Product Unique

If you plan to create and sell a product, work out in your mind what you can do to give that product some unique personal touch that will serve as a trademark and make it stand out.

When one teenager started her own small business taking orders for high-fashion doll clothes, she pinned her own trademark—a tiny corsage of matching artificial flowers—on every outfit she made.

Display Your Products and Advertise Your Service

The youthful creator of high style for dolls got her business going—and you can take your cue from this—by advertising her products and displaying and taking orders for them whenever and wherever she could.

She got an excellent start by donating some of her doll clothes to bazaars, fairs and fund-raising projects. Then, as she saw how well the clothes sold, she got into the habit of taking—along with her donations—some 3 x 5 index cards on which she typed her name, address, telephone, and price list for the doll clothes she made. As she left her donations at the fair, she'd ask the people in charge of the fair to display her cards, with one or two not-to-be-sold sample garments, *after* her donations were sold. In that way her advertising never interfered with the fair's profits —but potential customers could call her.

There are other advertising methods. You can take samples of products you'd like to sell to shops and restaurants in your vicinity. As you show your products to the people in charge, inquire about the possibility of having them sold at the shop or restaurant or having orders placed through the shop. Since it's highly possible, however, that one shop might want an exclusive on the product, begin with your first-choice shop or restaurant.

Use every possible method to let people know of your service. Run small advertisements in your local paper, or make up mimeographed cards or announcements describing your business and distribute them where people will see them. Tell your friends and acquaintances what you're doing and ask them to tell their friends and acquaintances. In addition, talk to the people who are leaders of the community organizations in your area and ask them if they'll announce your service at their meetings. Finally, make good use of free bulletin boards in supermarkets or other spots in your area by posting a card announcing your service there.

Figure Out Your Fees

Before plunging into any business or special service take sufficient time to figure out appropriate prices or fees for your services.

You can decide on fees by determining how much your time is worth, what your expenses will be, and how much profit you'll need to make the business or service worth while. While you're doing this, compare your prices with the prices of similar products or services to see how they line up. Also, ask people with business experience and judgment to give you advice.

Consider Getting a Partner

If developing a business or service of your own seems like too much to do alone, consider the possibility of adding your talent or skill to someone else's and starting a partnership. Very often two people's skills are just the right combination.

Two fifteen-year-old girls with the reputation of being the best dressed girls in their school have paid their way to that reputation with a party service they've run for two years. One of the girls likes to organize games, and the other likes to work in the kitchen, so the service run by this twosome allows plenty of room for both girls to do the jobs they love best. Their parties are for children under twelve, and their telephones ring regularly with calls from local mothers who are happy to turn over the party responsibilities to them for a fee.

"And the best thing about this service," one of the girls said, "is the fact that it's giving us both ideas for our future careers. We're thinking of taking home economics and then starting our own catering business."

Not every part-time job or personal business service is a dress rehearsal for the future, of course. But now and then it happens, just as it happened to Sandy Schippers and Arthur Taylor, and so it may happen to you.

Paying Hobbies

Another way to find a career is through a paying hobby.

Gladys Shelley, a vivacious and highly successful song writer who currently cashes big checks for her lyrics and music, used to cash checks—smaller ones—in her growing up years, from her joint hobbies of writing poetry and giving younger children piano and dancing lessons.

Photographer Victor Keppler, whose photographs have appeared in practically every magazine and newspaper in the United States, Canada, South America and Europe, practiced picture-taking while working his way through both high school and college. Albert Martinez, who lives on the island of Curaçao, turned his teenage hobby of fishing into a commercial career in which he now catches tropical fish and ships them to the United States, Denmark, Austria, Germany and Holland. And Phil Romayne, the spectacular adagio skating star, began skating for fun when he was eleven. At thirteen he started to make his skating pay, in experience and money, by taking odd jobs around skating rinks.

Enoch Light, founder and managing director of Command Records, got his start through his hobby of music. In his early teens Light took violin and piano lessons. Then, in high school, he organized a band to play at school dances. With the money he earned from this he paid for part of his college education, which in the beginning was aimed at a pre-med course.

His hobby of music took over again when, while studying at Johns Hopkins University, he organized another band. The money he earned from that helped pay college expenses, but the success of his band put music in his blood for good. After graduation, Light decided to pursue a musical career.

It was a good decision. Light won international fame as a band leader and later became known in the record industry as the man who revolutionized stereo recording techniques.

Music is a favorite when it comes to paying hobbies!

In Chicago, three teenagers in the Schneider family accumulate part-time revenue in a seven-piece musical combo called the "Dukes of Kent." Nineteen-year-old Kent plays the trumpet, and his sisters Nancy, fifteen, and Janet, thirteen, play the banjo and guitar respectively.

The four Topper boys of Dallas, Texas, are studying with a professional jazz musician. Like Light, they plan to help pay for education by cashing checks from their hobby.

In Trenton, New Jersey, Susan Savage clowned her way through her teens and earned her share of extra cash by performing with her father, Walt Savage, whose hobby is also clowning. Susan, whose clown name was "Candy," performed at birthday parties, acted in shows for children's groups, and did advertising or promotional work for businessmen.

Don't Let Working Interfere with Your School Work

If you organize yourself and make time count, work shouldn't interfere, but in the event that school plus work is too much you'll be the first to know, as you see your grades start to slip and feel sleep go down the drain. Remember, school work must always come first!

What About Working to Support a Car?

If you're planning a job to support a car, put on two thinking caps!

A study made by the Allstate Insurance Companies, in cooperation with thirty selected high schools, was specifically designed to throw a searchlight on the academic, driving, and social habits of twenty thousand Junior and Senior students. Results showed that holding a job to support a car adversely affected teenagers' attitudes toward school. Besides, curtailment of study time created by the job-car combination led to a vicious circle. Of students spending $6.00 or more per week on car support only one per cent were A students, but among those who spent $3.00 or less, the ratio of A students was four times as high.

Why knock yourself out in your teens? There's too much ahead in the future! But somewhere between the Knock Yourself Out way of life and the Take It Easy way of life, there's the Happy Medium way. It's to your advantage to start earning money now through part-time jobs, services, or hobbies. Here are ten good reasons:

1. A job, business, or paying hobby is a learning experience you can't duplicate anywhere else in life. The "College of Hard Knocks" was the most important school for many highly successful people in the past.

2. It's a project from which you gain financially, because you learn the value of money when the money that comes and goes is your own. You also learn the value of time as you budget it through necessity.

3. A job teaches you to be reliable—an important foundation in the building of a successful future.

4. It helps you respect yourself. You think more of yourself when you can offer something somebody wants to buy.

5. It shows you how to evaluate your strengths and weaknesses in an employer's eye.

6. It provides you with "try-out" experience in the give and take of the working world, and gives you a chance to work with many different types of people.

7. It gives you knowledge and experience that may someday knit together with other knowledge and experience to land you a good job.

8. It's a ticket to the main act of your future because it shows you in a practical way (a) what you like to do, (b) what you can do, (c) what the business world thinks of you, and (d) what you'll need to do to make a success of yourself.

9. In some cases it gives you an "in" with a specific employer or business and makes it easier for you to get a job after you finish school.

One high school girl whose main interest was art got an after-school and Saturday job in the advertising section of a department store. When she graduated from high school and was ready for a full-time job, she had an opportunity to become a full-fledged commercial artist in the department store because of her previous experience and job performance.

10. Finally, in the words of an industrial psychologist, Dr. Mortimer R. Feinberg, who is President of BFS Psychological Associates and Associate Professor of the Baruch School at the City College of New York:

"Suitable work, even on a part-time basis, can provide a teenager with an opportunity to test his mettle away from mother's watchful eye and father's protection.

"I believe, further, that work can be an essential ingredient of the socialization process. The working youngster can learn the importance of responsibility, self-discipline, and respect for authority that he may resist at home. As one youngster confessed to me, 'Last term when I had a cold I'd simply stay home from school. Now, with a library job, I go to school and just make certain to show up at work with an extra package of Kleenex.'"

In order to show up at work, however, you need to find a job. So let's go job hunting next.

4

A Job Hunt That Wins

You can get a job in your teens if your job hunt can beat the competition!

Today there are more young people seeking jobs than ever before in history. In fact, one-half of the people in our population were born during or after World War II! Eighty-five million of them are younger than twenty-five. Forty-one million are children under ten. And about twenty-seven million are between ten and eighteen. Consequently, when you're getting your start for your future during the next ten years, at least twenty-five million other young Americans will be coming into the labor market to do the same thing.

To compete, you must be in the know about job-getting

techniques. So study the next three chapters, not only for the part-time jobs you want now but also for the full-time and summer jobs you'll want later on. You'll use these techniques all your life.

Tracking Down Job Possibilities and Leads

Here are ten good tickets for tracking down job leads:

1. Compile a list of possible employers by going through your classified telephone directory and copying down the names of people and places most likely to need the type of work you can do. Then get in touch with them to see whether they have openings or needs.

2. Let your school guidance or placement counselor know you're in the market for a job. Employers often notify schools when they're in the market for help.

3. Read the want ads in the paper as regularly as you eat pizza or drink coke.

4. Tell everyone you know you're available for work.

5. Visit the office of your nearest state employment service to see whether there are openings you could fill. This free employment service is equipped to help young people find jobs. It also offers counseling and testing services.

When you go to a state employment office it's a good idea to take with you at least two clean, crisp copies of your job résumé. (There will be full information on preparing résumés in Chapter V.) On arriving at the state employment office, report to the reception desk. The receptionist in charge will determine your needs and refer you to the staff member best able to assist you. When you go to the office, be prepared to specify the type of job you can do and what hours you can work.

6. Go to the YMCA's or YWCA's in your area, since they often offer help to young people looking for job opportunities.

7. Talk to the heads of your Chamber of Commerce, as

well as to the heads of such service clubs as Kiwanis International, Lions, and Rotary. Doing this will be time well spent, because service clubs occasionally set up special projects to assist young people who want to find jobs.

8. After you've made these visits, go to personnel departments of large firms in your area and see whether they accept applications from a person of your age. If they do, put your application on file. Even if they have no openings when you apply, it's possible they'll call you if openings arise.

9. Go through daily and weekly papers in your area and look for items about new businesses or industries preparing to open in your vicinity. Since most of these places will be in the market for employees, a letter of application to them may put you in line for a job.

10. Finally, place a "Situation Wanted" ad in the paper. In the ad, state your qualifications, the work you can do, the hours you can work, and the telephone number at which you can be reached. (You might also add, as a lure, "Reasonable rates.")

Sample "Situation Wanted" Ads

SITUATION WANTED—FEMALE

TYPING STUDENT, age 16, with speed, accuracy and a good telephone voice seeks part-time office job. Can work 3:30 to 5:30 daily plus Saturday mornings. Call 111-2222

SITUATION WANTED—MALE

ODD-JOBS MAN, age 17, with car and willingness to work at menial jobs seeks odd jobs for businesses or private homes on weekends. Call 111-2222

SITUATION WANTED—FEMALE

DOG WALKER with love for dogs will walk and feed for business people and those confined at home. Available before or after school, depending on your location. Call 111-2222

SITUATION WANTED—MALE

AMBITIOUS HIGH SCHOOL SENIOR desires job as counter man, cashier, stock boy or check-out boy. Can work full-time Saturday and Sunday. Part-time afternoons or evenings during week. Call 111-2222

Beat the "No Experience" Battle

Actually, no one expects you to be weighed down by too much experience at this point in your life! Besides, you do have some stashed away. There's no one, anywhere, who hasn't piled up some experience as a result of school and community life.

Consequently, you can combat this "no experience" worry in three ways.

First, aim your job-hunting shots whenever possible at employers who advertise, "No experience necessary."

Second, build your job hunt on your achievements in your school and community life. As you'll see in the next chapter, you can build an entire job hunt on your educational attainments, talents and interests, community service, and desire to learn. Your "See Yourself" tests will help you on this.

Third, turn your inexperience into an asset when employers make a point of the "no experience" angle. Point out gracefully that because you're facing your first job you're anxious to do things the way your employer wants them done instead of insisting on doing them the way you

did in past jobs. "This isn't the first shop I've worked in,
you know. I know how to do things myself!" is not a re-
mark calculated to hold a job.

Smart Viewpoints on Part-Time Jobs

Our world is a large one, so the more things you know
about it the more you'll have to contribute to your future
career. Consequently, it doesn't really matter at this point
whether your present job is within your major field of
interest or just any job you could get. People have arrived
both ways.

Richard Aimesbury, for example, a top restaurateur
and director of New York's colorful Paul Revere Tavern
and Chop House, used the first approach and built a
career in food management by starting with a job as a bell
hop when he was a teenager. From that point on he
geared all of his jobs, as well as his education, to learning
about the food management field.

Famous artist Norman Rockwell took any job he could
get, from the time he was fifteen, to earn money for his art
lessons.

The approach you take will probably depend to a great
extent upon what you can get in part-time jobs. If you find
you can get something that ties in with your future job
field, you're lucky. But if you're not that lucky, and can
get only something far afield, you'll still be doing your
future a favor to take what you can get. Even short terms
of employment will be invaluable experience.

If your greatest ambition right now is to get a part-time
job in your main field of interest, however, it won't cost
you any more to look for jobs in that field first. But you'll
stand a greater chance of getting a job if you sort yourself
out and try to determine these four things:

What specific services could I perform in this field?

Is there a need in my area for these services? (To determine this, watch the Help Wanted ads in the paper.)

How well qualified am I to perform these services?

What's my main reason for wanting to do them now? (Along with your wish to earn money, you also, if you're smart, want to do these things because they'll give you a chance to put your abilities and skills to work and develop yourself further.)

You'll need a Social Security card regardless of your age, so get your number from your local post office or Social Security office. You can find your nearest Social Security office in the telephone book under the "United States government" listing.

Begin your job hunt by buying a pack of 3 x 5 index cards. Then make out a card for each job lead you find, whether you intend to follow up that lead now or in the future. Indicate on each card the name, address, and phone number of each individual, firm, or business. Also write down the source of your lead. If you know the name of a person to reach at the firm, mark that on the card, too. Later you'll use these cards to write down dates and notations whenever you write or telephone a firm. Also when you're fortunate enough to get an interview, use the cards to write the date of the interview, the name of the person who interviewed you, and the outcome of the interview.

Starting your job hunt will also involve answering Help Wanted ads, writing application letters and presenting résumés.

It will involve preparing yourself for interviews, putting yourself over during interviews, filling out application blanks, and taking tests, all of which we'll cover in this and the next two chapters. But before we go into these approaches, let's point out some wrong approaches noted by many employers.

Actually, it's almost as important in job hunting to know what not to do as it is to know what to do, so here—from the mouths of employers—are some job-hunting peeves:

"One of the mistakes teenagers commonly make is either overselling or underselling themselves."

"Too many of them job hunt without an appointment."

"They arrive without résumés and are insufficiently prepared for an interview."

"They dress incorrectly and have no idea of what they want to do or what kind of job they're applying for."

"They don't show enough concern for an employer's interest. Instead, they're completely concerned with their own interests."

"They need to be better trained in self-expression. They often have nothing to say."

"Instead of applying for a job on their own, they job-hunt in pairs with friends and relatives. This is always a mistake because it makes them look insecure. It also makes it awkward for an employer to hire just one person out of the twosome."

"They apply for jobs for which they're unsuited and for which they have no skill."

"They act indifferent in an interview and show no real interest in a job while they're being interviewed."

"They're unrealistic about beginners' wages and they show distaste for what they're offered."

"They demand too much and refuse to see their own limitations because of their age."

"Some of them are undependable. If they don't feel like showing up for a scheduled interview they don't even bother to telephone to say they won't be there."

"And even worse," concluded one employer, "they don't always follow through on commitments when they say they're taking a job. Just last week, for example, I hired a high school Senior to work as a receptionist and typist after school. But she didn't arrive as she'd promised she would for the first three days she was due to work. Finally I telephoned her to see what had happened. When I reached her she told me nothing had happened. She'd just decided, after all, that she didn't want a job!"

Though these are only a few of the things employers gripe about, they're a large enough assortment to give you a full-sized view of the wrong approach.

Answering Help Wanted Ads

Your first try-out for a part-time job may begin with Help Wanted ads.

To get in line for answering ads, make it your everyday habit to go over all the Help Wanted advertising in all the papers you can accumulate. Check each ad that you feel you could answer, and then analyze each marked ad and list what each one specifically wants. Also list as well as you can what each ad tells you about the employer and his business, the type of work, the location, and so forth. With this squared away, you're ready to answer some job ads.

If the ad specifies a phone number to call, decide before you place the call what questions you're likely to be asked. Possible questions will be inquiries about your skills, experience, age, and plans for getting back and forth to work. By jotting down your answers to all of them in advance, you'll have clear answers in your own mind and be ready for a quick answer when the question is posed.

Once your thoughts are collected and you're ready to place the telephone call, be absolutely sure you speak clearly. This makes an important first impression.

Along with speaking clearly, remember to indicate, as soon as someone answers the phone, what job ad you're answering and where and when you saw the ad. This is important, because many employers often advertise more than one job at once.

In the following chapter we'll talk about the right techniques for answering job ads by letter.

5

A Letter That Lures

HELP WANTED

CLERK—For drugstore. Part-time.
Mon.-Thurs. evenings, 5-9 P.M.
Driver's license necessary.
Write to Box 111, *The Daily Star.*

WHEN Help Wanted ads give a box number, as the one above does, make your salutation "Gentlemen" or "Dear Sir," since you have no way of knowing the name of the person or company you're addressing.

As for the letter itself, make it brief and to the point. Say what you have to say in clear, simple English. Use plain white bond paper (typing paper is a good size) and mail the letter in a plain, legal-size envelope.

Unless you're asked to answer in your own handwriting,

type your letter or have someone type it for you. If this is absolutely impossible, write the letter in ink. Get your letter in the mail as soon as possible, too, because a job won't wait while you wait to write. Someone else will get it.

When you're ready to write your letter you'll find a sample letter to use as a guide on page 58. Later, you'll find a sample résumé on page 64. Certain things will go into the letter and certain things will go into the résumé. But let's look at the letter first.

Writing the Letter

In the *first* paragraph, identify the ad you're answering just as you would if you were answering by telephone.

In the *second* paragraph get into the body of the letter by appealing to the self-interests of the employer who placed the ad. You can determine these self-interests by going over the things for which the ad specifically asks. Once you've determined these things, tailor your qualifications and skills to fit the specifications. Whenever possible include a concrete example of one of your qualifications in action. You might use one example in your letter and another one in your résumé.

In the *third* paragraph describe your working experience so far. If you have no working experience, pinpoint specific experiences you have had in school or volunteer work, and show, by a concrete example, how these experiences would help in the job for which you're applying.

In the *fourth* paragraph mention your age and education and the résumé you're enclosing.

Finally, conclude the letter by indicating your interest in the job and requesting an interview. Give clear information on where you can be reached by letter or phone. Then end the letter with a "thank you."

Here is a sample letter to follow as a guide for writing your own. This one—a job-winning letter, incidentally—was written in answer to the ad appearing at the beginning of this chapter.

Street Address
Town and State
Date

Box 111
The Daily Star
Wilmington, Pennsylvania

Dear Sir:

This letter is in answer to the advertisement for a part-time drugstore clerk which appeared in *The Daily Star* on March 1, 19_____. I am particularly interested in this job because I'm planning a career as a pharmacist.

Because of this interest I am especially anxious for a chance to help in a drugstore doing routine tasks. I have had my driver's license for one year, and I'm used to driving in all kinds of situations and weather. I always manage to get to my destination, too. Last summer, for example, while driving my family on an emergency trip to our vacation cottage I was the only driver in the area who didn't get stuck during a rain which nearly washed out the dirt road.

So far, my working experience has included summer employment as a stock boy between my Sophomore and Junior years. I have also sold and delivered magazines and worked after school as a chore boy.

I am seventeen years old and a Junior in Wadsworth High School. Further qualifications and experience are listed in my résumé. I hope this letter indicates to you how happy I would be to work for you. May I come in for an interview whenever it's convenient with you? You can reach me or leave a message by calling 777-1111 or by writing me at the above address. Thank you for your consideration.

Sincerely yours,
Your Signature in Ink
Sam Smith

Besides answering job ads, you'll be writing application letters to other firms that might have jobs available. You won't have box numbers for these letters, though, so—whenever possible—try to find out the name of the person to whom you should direct your letter before you write it. A telephone call to the firms themselves will get you this information.

Essentially, your other job application letters will be similar to those you write in answer to job ads. But since there's no need to specify a job ad in these letters, you can start right out taking the employer's view of things and suggesting specific jobs you can do for him. In addition, the beginning paragraph should also leave the job door open by mentioning that you'd be interested in filling other needs, too. Include, also, your reasons for wanting to work. And if you're writing at the suggestion of a mutual friend, mention that friend.

In the body of the letter specify briefly your past experience in summer and part-time jobs, volunteer work, school or extracurricular work. Highlight one specific thing that serves as a good success story and shows your past performances. Save another success story for your résumé. And don't decide, incidentally, that you haven't a success story. Everyone has some!

In the conclusion of your letter state your age and education. Mention the inclusion of your résumé, and ask for an interview. Then end with a gracious "thank you."

Sometimes at the end of your letter you'll find it's a practical idea to suggest a specific date for an interview. When you do this, follow up your suggestion by saying you'll telephone ahead of time to inquire about the convenience of this date. That makes people pay attention to a letter they might otherwise ignore.

Here's how one boy wrote his job application letter.

                                        Street Address
                                        Town and State
                                        Date

Mr. Louis Manning, Owner
Pine Tree Diner
Pine Tree Road
Orville, Oregon

Dear Mr. Manning:

Each time my family and I visit your diner for Sunday dinner I've noticed how many people arrive for this meal each week. I've also noticed how much your regular help has to keep on the run to do all the jobs that need to be done. Because of this I'd like to apply for a part-time job as bus boy and general helper during your busiest hours. I can work all day Saturdays and Sundays.

I'm particularly anxious to work for you because, after I graduate from high school, I hope to get into the food service field. With this in mind, I want to start learning the business from the bottom up as soon as possible.

For the past few years I've worked as a kitchen or dining room helper at most of the church dinners our church runs. On the few occasions I haven't volunteered my help, people have come and asked me to help, so I feel they like the way I work. I also feel the experience gained in this work would help me to help you. Except for a few paid jobs doing chores for people, my other experiences so far have all been volunteer work, school and extracurricular activities. But whenever I've worked as a chore boy I've always been asked back to do other jobs.

I'm sixteen years old and a Sophomore in high school. The attached résumé will give you more of my background and experience. At your convenience I'd like very much to stop at your diner and talk to you. I can be reached at the above address or by telephoning 111-2222. I'm wondering, though, if it would be possible to talk with you next Monday or Tuesday, April 10 or 11. May I telephone you to find out?

Thank you very much for considering me.

> Sincerely,
> *Your Own Signature*
> Roy Wyckoff

Once you have your letter drafted, go over it with a fine-tooth comb to be sure it reads well and expresses a touch of your personality. Work on each paragraph until each one is simple, crisp and sincere. Often, reading the letter aloud helps you achieve this effect. Whenever possible, show your letter to someone whose opinion you respect and have that person check it before you send it out.

While you're doing these things, you can put your letter to the following test to see whether it's the right ticket for a job.

1. Is the letter neat and attractively presented on plain white paper?

2. Have you spelled each word correctly and avoided crossed-out and inserted words?

3. Have you double checked the address to make sure it's correct?

4. Have you signed the letter?

5. Have you left out all mention of salary (since that will come up in the interview)?

6. Have you given concrete examples of what you can do instead of making general statements?

7. Have you designated the job or work for which you're applying?

8. Have you angled your letter toward things an employer would want in an employee?

9. Have you written it in a simple and readable style and avoided unnecessary words and information?

10. Have you ended it with a question as a pitch for hearing from the employer or getting in touch with him yourself?

In order to get a few answers, you have to send out many letters, because whenever you send out cold letters there's always the gamble you'll hit employers when they have no need. Beyond this, there's the chance that someone who plans to answer you out of courtesy will push your letter aside because of the pressure of work.

You never know, though, when a letter you send out will start to work for you long after you give up—especially if you're like one young boy who wrote two hundred letters to get a part-time job.

At the time he sent out the two hundred letters none of them yielded him a job, so he took whatever work he could find. Then, one year later, a letter came offering him an interview for a job. And that was because the boy's original job application letter had made such a good impression that the head of the firm had kept it in sight for a year so he'd know where to find the boy!

Résumés

A résumé, as you probably know, is a well-organized presentation of (1) what you can do, (2) what you have done, (3) what you know, (4) who you are, and (5) what kind of job you'd like.

When you prepare yours, you'll need to remember four general rules:

1. Don't use carbon copies. If you need more copies than you can type, get them mimeographed. (When you get older, though, and start your full-time career, you'll need photo offset résumés, not mimeographed ones.)

2. Use plain white paper and type on one side only. 8½ x 11 is a good size.

3. Try to keep the résumé to one page—though this is a rule that has leeway if you need more space.

4. Present your résumé in a narrative style that tells your story in a readable way. But each word must count. Don't be needlessly wordy.

How Can Students Prepare Résumés?

When students are ready to prepare their résumés, they often ask, "If I have to include my experience in a job application letter what have I left to put in a résumé? I'm afraid I'll repeat myself," or, "How can I write a résumé when I've never worked?"

As indicated earlier, the answer to the first question is to put part of your experience in your letter and part of your experience in your résumé. One good success story, or concrete example, in your letter and another one in your résumé is all anyone expects of you. You don't have to worry about a certain amount of repetition, either, because some details—such as your telephone number, age, and desired job—will be repeated. That's to be expected.

Here is a sample résumé that you can follow if you've never worked before, or if your working experience is limited. Use the format as a guide, and fill in the things that pertain to you. The physical format is on the next page.

RÉSUMÉ FORMAT FOR STUDENTS

Name: _____   Picture if one
                                is used
Street: _____

City: _____

Telephone: _____

Age: _____

Social Security Number: _____

JOB WANTED

_____

_____

EXPERIENCE

Worked in _____

From _____ to _____

In my job I _____

**ADDITIONAL EXPERIENCES IN COMMUNITY SERVICE,
SCHOOL, HOBBIES, EXTRACURRICULAR WORK**

_____

_____

ASSETS, ABILITIES, AND MAIN INTERESTS

_____

_____

EDUCATION

_____

_____

REFERENCES

_____

_____

PERSONAL DATA

_____

_____

Fill-In Material for Résumé

JOB WANTED

Specify here the type of job or work you're seeking.

Experience

If you've worked at any summer, part-time or temporary jobs, start with the latest job and list the businesses or organizations for which you worked, the job classification you had and the dates you held the job. Describe briefly what you did in each job and include specific examples of your accomplishments that you didn't include in your job application letter.

If you've never had actual working experience, use this section to indicate a school or community experience that would have some bearing on the job for which you're applying. For example, if you're applying for a part-time job in sales, the fact that you sold more subscriptions to your school newspaper than anyone else would be highly pertinent.

Additional Experiences in Community Service, School, Hobbies, Extracurricular Activities

To sell yourself at your best, list everything in these categories that tells the story of you and shows what kind of person you are. Then narrow down your list to the best-selling points before you prepare the final copy of your résumé.

Assets, Abilities, and Main Interests

If you're really short on material, list items that come under these categories and turn them into selling points by giving examples of them in action. Also indicate how you hope to use and develop them further in a job.

Education

Specify your present grade in school, the course you're taking, your best subjects, and any academic honor you've received, unless you've already mentioned these things.

References

After asking two people who know your abilities and character if you may use their names as references, list their names, addresses, and phone numbers here.

Personal Data

Under this section list:

Date of birth

Physical condition

Height and weight, if that has bearing on the job

If you're a boy over eighteen, subject to entering the armed forces, mention your standing with the draft board.

Whenever the subject of résumés comes up you'll hear a lot of pros and cons on whether or not to include your photograph. A good picture does help to establish you as a person and stamp an image of you in an employer's mind. When you use a picture, however, make it a head and shoulders one and paste it at the top right-hand corner of the résumé. Boys should be dressed in a white shirt, tie and jacket. Girls should be dressed in a suit, simple blouse or dress.

Before presenting your résumé, go over it with the same fine-tooth comb you used to check your job application letter. When possible, check the résumé with someone else. Also, check it with the following "See Yourself" Résumé Quiz:

1. Is your résumé neat and well-typed, with all margins even?

2. Is it organized, and spaced so that the presentation is attractive and easy to read?

3. Does it specify the type of job you want?

4. Does it sell you by showing the services you can perform?

5. Is it alive with one or two good success stories?

In addition to mailing copies of your résumé with your job application letters, you should also take résumés with you when you go on interviews.

6

A Win-the-Job Interview

PREPARING the right kind of interview is one of your most important steps for both a job and a future because in the fifteen or twenty minutes you have for an interview you have to get across four things: your background and experience; your personality, intelligence, appearance, manner and speech; your interest in the company; your reason for wanting to work for this company.

A necessity that's so terribly basic it shouldn't even need to be mentioned is to make an appointment. Yet employers say that too many young people fail to do this.

Once the appointment is made, the next preparatory step is to write down the time and place of the interview. Get the full name of the company to which you're applying and try to find out all you can about it. Whenever you can, get the name of the person who will interview you and check on the pronunciation of that name.

With these details behind you, figure out the answers to the questions you're most likely to be asked during the interview. Doing this will put you in line to make a better impression.

Possible questions you'll be asked will be:

> What can I do for you?
> Tell me about yourself.
> Why are you interested in working for us?
> What schools have you attended?
> What are your favorite subjects?
> Why do you like these subjects?
> In what subjects do you get the best grades?
> In what activities do you participate?

Other Questions

Here are some other favorite questions applicable to junior and senior high school students, from a New York Life Insurance Company report based on a survey by Frank S. Endicott, Director of Placement, Northwestern University:

What are your future vocational plans?

How do you spend your spare time? What are your hobbies?

What type of work interests you most?

Have you ever worked before? If so, how did you get your job, and why did you leave?

How do you spend your vacations while in school?

What do you know about our company?

What qualifications have you that make you feel you'll be successful?

What are your ideas on salary?

How do you feel about your family?

Are you interested in sports? As an observer? As a participant?

How do you rank in your class in school?

Why do you think you would like this particular type of job?

What is your father's occupation?

Tell me about your home life.

Do you prefer working with others or by yourself?

Who are your best friends?

What kind of boss do you prefer?

Can you take instructions?

How did previous employers treat you?

What have you learned from some of the jobs you've held?

Can you get recommendations from previous employers?

Do you feel you have done the best scholastic work of which you're capable?

How long do you expect to work?

Have you ever had any difficulty in getting along with your fellow students and your teachers?

What's the source of your spending money?

Have you saved any money?

Do you attend church?

Do you like routine work?

Do you like regular hours?

What do you think is your major weakness?

Are you eager to please?

What do you do to keep in good physical condition?

How do you usually spend Sunday?

Have you ever had any serious illness or injury?

What type of books have you read?

What are your special abilities?

Are you willing to do overtime work?

Do you think that grades should be considered by employers?

What have you done that shows initiative and willingness to work?

You'll never have to answer all these questions in one interview, of course, but chances are you'll face some of them. Prepare your answers ahead of time so you won't be saying "Uh" or "Ah."

A Practice Interview

A "practice" interview at home is another important part of your preparation. You can't learn all your lines ahead of time, of course, since you don't know what you'll be asked. But you can increase your poise and presentation for an interview by rehearsing what you think you'll be asked.

One good way to rehearse is to swallow your self-consciousness and ask a friend or a parent to go through a practice interview with you. If this is impossible, use a mirror as your helper.

With a person or a mirror before you, go through several practice interviews, using combinations of the questions you're likely to be asked. When you find that a question stops you, make a mental note to do more work on figuring out the answer.

Make your practice session a real dress rehearsal, too, by actually dressing for the interview and walking into the room, greeting your helper, and sitting down as though the whole thing were for real. Don't make a comedy of it, either, no matter how much you want to ham things up!

Dressing for the Interview

Dressing for an interview begins with personal cleanliness, which is all-important, even if it seems too routine to mention. This means a bath or shower, clean underwear, a shampoo, a deodorant and a mouthwash before you leave home. One boy who thought he knew everything lost the job he wanted as a kitchen helper in a summer hotel before he even opened his mouth to ask for it when one look at his nails—black as mourning around the edges—caused an interviewer to rule him out for a job with foods.

Spotless clothes are the next necessity. Everything should be spanking-clean, freshly pressed, and appropriate in style and taste. White should be immaculately white. Shoes should be polished. And lifts on the shoes should be straight.

For girls, stockings and high-heeled shoes with a simple dress, a skirt and blouse that match, or a suit, are good choices. If gloves are appropriate put on a pair of clean white ones just before the interview. Jewelry should be at a minimum. So should perfume and make-up. Eliminate a head scarf if you're tempted to wear one. Avoid beat-up car coats, jackets and raincoats and wear a coat that coordinates well with your outfit. If you must wear a short coat, make sure that the skirt or dress showing under it complements the coat as attractively as possible.

Boys on the job trail need to be equally well dressed. An always appropriate choice is a suit or a pair of slacks with a jacket that complements the slacks. A white shirt, tie and socks that blend, and a spotlessly clean pocket handkerchief make up the rest of the outfit.

Special tips for boys include (1) a fresh haircut, (2) hair grooming aid to keep hair in place, (3) clean hands, (4) trimmed nails, and (5) a close-shaven face.

Special tips for girls include (1) a clean, uncluttered

purse, (2) hair that's brushed and shining and arranged
in a simple, neat coiffure, and (3) well-manicured nails
with light polish. To be on the safe side leave your eye
make-up at home, since many employers have definite
ideas about that. "What are the girls trying to do?" is one
complaint. "They look more prepared for Halloween than
they do for getting a job."

Finally, don't spoil your appearance by taking a "tote"
bag to an interview so you can fill it as you go with books,
magazines, newspapers, packages, and boxes. When you
do this you look like a cluttered and overloaded Christmas
tree and you spoil your appearance and grooming.

When your interview day arrives you may feel edgy
and nervous, but that's entirely normal. Almost everyone
feels that way. Put your nervousness behind you as well as
you can and plan to arrive at the designated place at least
fifteen minutes early. It's better for you to be kept waiting
than it is for you to keep an interviewer waiting. Have a
supply of both pencils and pens in your pocket or purse.
And be sure that your regular pen—plus a spare pen—is
supplied with ink. Be equally sure that you have a small
notebook tucked away somewhere so you can jot down
any necessary notes.

Filling Out Application Blanks

Application forms will vary at different places, but they'll
all ask for many of the same basic things.

Be prepared ahead of time with data and dates on your
training, abilities and experience, plus your social security
number and references. If you can't rely on your memory,
put this information on a card that you can carry with
you. Then you can copy the information from the card as

you fill out the form. By all means, answer each question honestly. Read directions before you write, and use ink to fill out the form.

Follow directions exactly and fill in each space in which you're asked to supply an answer. If a question does arise that doesn't apply to you or your background, specify that in the space provided so that the finished application form won't look as though you overlooked some questions.

Take extra copies of your résumé (see p. 64) to interviews. Then, if you run up against an application form that hasn't the kind of questions you can answer, you can attach your résumé to the form. A paper clip or pocket stapler will put you in business for this.

Job Tests

After you fill out an application form there's always the possibility you'll be asked to take some tests before the interview. There's no reason for these tests to throw you, though, so don't let your nerves be the winners. Interviewers know you're nervous, so they often make allowances for that if you do a reasonably good job otherwise.

When you're applying for an office job, tests will usually include a routine test on typing and shorthand. Fifty words a minute in typing is generally acceptable. Ninety to one hundred words a minute is often the expected in shorthand. In some places you may be asked to take a letter at one of three speeds and then set up and type the letter with a limited number of errors. Chances are also very great that you may run into simple I.Q. tests and general aptitude tests, as well as tests in English, spelling, vocabulary, punctuation, filing, and simple arithmetic.

The test administrators themselves will give you a thorough explanation of what you're to do, a short practice exercise, and a chance to ask questions. Most of the time you'll find that test administrators are friendly, relaxed people. And, generally, tests aren't the whole factor in whether or not you get a job. They're used in conjunction with other factors, including your experience and qualifications.

The Interview

Here are some tips for putting yourself over during the interview:

1. Take your cue from your interviewer. If he moves to shake hands, shake hands. Stand until he tells you to sit. And for your job's sake don't smoke or chew gum.

2. Look alert and interested. When you're asked to sit down, don't sit so close to the edge of your chair that you look tense and ready to take off. But, at the same time, don't sit so far back that you look ready to fall asleep.

3. Establish eye contact with your interviewer. Smile at appropriate intervals so you show yourself as a friendly person.

4. Act calm instead of nervous. If you're a finger picker, stop being picky. If you're a handkerchief twister, keep your handkerchief out of sight.

5. Speak up when you're asked to answer questions. Don't act as though you're afraid of your voice, yourself and the interview as a whole.

6. Be factual and sincere about yourself in a quiet way without flaunting the red flag of conceit.

7. Be brief and to the point. Stick to the subject at hand instead of going off on unnecessary tangents.

8. Suggest a specific type of job you can do instead of saying in a general and vague way, "I'll take anything."

9. Keep your confidence in yourself at a high level, even when you're unfortunate enough to run into a domineering, unfeeling interviewer whose manner intimidates you.

Unfortunately, every one of us runs into this type of interviewer sometimes. So my favorite advice for this is to keep your confidence where it belongs by visualizing the woman who makes you feel like this the way she'd look in a mussy housecoat with her hair up in rollers and her make-up in the drawer instead of on her face. When it's a man who intimidates you, think of him as unshaven and running around in a faded nightshirt!

10. Have a definite understanding as to what's required of you before you're hired. If you're hired, get an "Offer of Employment" from the firm, stating the type of work, the hours, and the salary that you may expect. You will need this "Offer of Employment" to get working papers.

11. Be alert for signs that the interview is completed. For example, pick up the cue when the interviewer folds your résumé, puts your application to one side of his desk, or says he's glad you came in. Make a move when you see this sign. Without seeming to take forever, gather your things together and leave quickly with a gracious "Thank you."

If everything you've read so far seems like a lot for a young boy or girl to offer, let me assure you that no one expects you to be the Boy (or Girl) Who Has Everything just to get a job. The important thing is to have some strong, shining qualities that show through your less shining ones. And if you have them, they'll show!

One young boy who was painfully shy went to a supermarket one day to ask for a job. As he asked very shyly about the possibility of after-school work, an architect who happened to be in the store overheard the conversation. While the man and the boy waited to see the person in charge, the architect asked the shy young man what school he attended, since the architect's firm was looking for a boy to work in the office after school.

When the boy answered that he was attending a vocational school and learning drafting, the architect snapped to attention. Then, as he talked to the boy and saw all the fine qualities that showed right through the shyness, he offered the boy a job interview at his office.

"Come down to our office and apply," he said. "We're in the market for a boy after school and you could learn as you work."

The shy young boy took the advice, went for an interview, got an after-school job as an office boy, and ultimately ended up not only getting valuable experience but also doing very well in a business that helped to shape his future career.

Thank-You Notes

Whatever the outcome of each interview is, keep the job door open by writing an employer a thank-you note for the time he spent with you. In the note, highlight a selling point for your services that came up in the interview. End the note by telling the employer you hope he'll keep you in mind.

The following letter can be your guide.

SAMPLE THANK-YOU LETTER

> Street address
> Town, State
> Date

Mr. John Engel
The Hamilton Ledger
Hamilton, Nebraska

Dear Mr. Engel:

Thank you so much for the interview you gave me today. After my conversation with you, your office seems a more interesting place to work than ever.

I observed your office routine while you interviewed me, and ever since I arrived home I have been thinking that there are other things I could do for you, in addition to typing. For instance, I noticed that you need someone to take the mail to the post office before the post office closes. Since I go by the post office regularly on my way home I could take on that job if I'm lucky enough to work for you. I'm also willing to do any other kind of errands or odd jobs that will help.

Thank you again for interviewing me. I hope you will keep me in mind.

> Sincerely,
> *Your Own Signature*
> Rita Howard

Your Telephone Number

What Do Employers Look for During an Interview?

Skills and qualifications are of first importance to a prospective employer, but here, in their own words, are some other things employers look for:

"I look for complete honesty, and I favor job applicants who speak directly and give straight, honest stories about themselves and their records."

"I like an assurance of industriousness and dependability."

"I like to see a willingness to work, and I'm impressed when a teenager doesn't emphasize how important short hours are."

"Speech, voice, good manners and a good attitude appeal to me. These qualities give me the feeling a job applicant will represent my business well."

"I look for young people who stand up straight instead of stooping all over as they hug their high school books."

"I look for spark and life, and I shy away from the lacklustre, blasé quality some teenagers have."

"The first thing I look at is the filled-out job application form. To me an impeccable application form means a person wants the job."

"I look for good manners, courtesy, and respect."

"I look for the person who asks a few intelligent questions about the job we're discussing. No job applicant should spend the whole interview time asking questions. But two or three intelligent questions at the proper time make an excellent impression."

"I look for the young person who's flexible and willing to make some compromises in order to meet business requirements. For instance, I don't like the girl who's willing to take only one job because that's the job that keeps her in contact with the boy who runs the elevator!"

Despite your best plans for an interview, some interviews go all wrong and you don't do well. That's human!

But no future is ruined by one mistake, so when you make mistakes, (1) file them under experience, (2) console yourself with the fact that everyone makes them sometimes, (3) refuse to be discouraged by something you can't change, and (4) move on to the next interview with a well-earned lesson behind you.

The worst experience the author had happened when she was a girl of eighteen, living in a small town and searching for a job in a city.

In order to go to her first interview she had to travel by train. But her confidence was doomed from the start, because, despite her fresh white gloves and her well-pressed navy blue dress, the rain that pelted down on the morning of the interview necessitated her leaving home with shiny black boots and her mother's new brown umbrella—since she didn't have one herself.

"Whatever you do," were her mother's last words,

"don't misplace my umbrella. I'll be furious if you lose it."

As luck would have it, the sun came out, and no one had boots or umbrellas; so the girl made up her mind that somehow she'd get rid of hers. Dropping the boots was easy. She simply threw them away and promised herself a new pair as soon as she got a job.

But the brown umbrella was different. Her mother had made that clear!

At best she knew she was stuck with it. But as she approached the office where she'd be interviewed she saw a crevice in a wall where she could hide the umbrella.

She thought the gods had smiled on her. But her happiness was short-lived because when the interviewer's chatty mother paid an unexpected call on her during the interview she mentioned the brown umbrella.

"It's a beautiful thing," she said, "and someone very foolishly left it in the hallway for anyone to steal."

She chattered about the umbrella as the young applicant filled out some forms. And every time she mentioned it, the girl knew she should say, "It's mine."

Then, finally, as the woman chattered like a long-playing phonograph record, her daughter told her to take it home, since no one seemed to want it.

The guilty one remembered her own mother's words, "I'll be furious if you lose it," and she knew that, job or no job, she had to get the umbrella back.

"It's mine," she squeaked in a high-C voice. "I borrowed it from my mother."

"Well, why didn't you say so?" the interviewer boomed. "Why didn't you speak up? How do you think you can get a job when you're as foolish as that!"

Because she had no answers, the girl didn't get the job. But she had learned something by making a bad mistake!

It's deflating when you feel you've done your best and still don't get a job. But there are several reasons why it can happen. To begin with, it's possible there were reasons beyond your control that made an employer say no to your job application. Perhaps there were no openings at the time you applied—or, if an opening had existed, it may have been filled just before you applied.

On the other hand, you may have been turned down because you slipped up on something you should have done in the interview. Be honest enough to face this possibility and prevent it from happening again. Refer to this chapter often, and check yourself on your interview conduct.

Whatever the reason, though, keep your courage up, since many people get many Noes before they hear "Yes." Refuse to be discouraged. There's a job for you somewhere if you try hard to find it.

When the happy day arrives, and you've found your part-time job, take the time to write or telephone a "thank you" to everyone whose time you took while looking for a job.

7

Make School Major While
Jobs Are Still Minor

DESPITE the part-time jobs you have, your main job right now is going to school. In fact, in our country, that is the most important job for every young person.

Why is school so important? There's really only one reason: In these days you need an education to succeed in both your job and future, and the easiest way to get it is to make use of your opportunities right now! If you don't, you'll have to work lots harder later on, since the learning opportunities you have now will never be available in quite the same way again. Vocationally speaking, many doors will be closed to you without a high school diploma.

At the present time, about as many people finish high school as finished eighth grade when your parents were young. About as many finish college now as finished high school in the past. Consequently, young people who try to enter the labor force without a high school diploma are the ones most likely to earn the least and to be unemployed. They're also the ones least likely to advance in their chosen field.

Because of the technological changes of this century, the future has little to offer the untrained, uneducated worker. Everywhere, new jobs requiring education are emerging in our automated, Space-Age world. At the same time, many jobs on farms and in factories that required little or no training are disappearing. Consequently, one of your greatest tickets to your future is a good high school education at which you do your best! Tests show that people who do the best work in school get the best breaks later on.

High school should be your first objective in developing a successful career for a number of reasons. Here are a few:

■ The courses on your schedule can open the door to interests you didn't know you had, as well as to interests you wouldn't discover if the courses weren't required.

Many of the courses you'll take will develop your mind and sharpen your intellectual curiosity—if you give them half a chance.

■ Some courses—such as health, stenography, and cooking—give you practical information and skills to help you in everyday living.

■ You'll develop your ability to think.

■ In school you will have experience in making decisions on your own.

■ In school you will learn to get along with people in classrooms, locker rooms, cafeterias, athletic activities and extracurricular activities, and this, as much as anything else, is an important part of your education. The New York State Employment Service reports that one of the most frequent reasons young people lose jobs is their inability to get along with others.

■ Your years in high school test and develop your sense of responsibility. Today's high schools are so crowded that no one can check on you constantly.

■ Your high school days show you your strengths and weaknesses in action. They indicate realistically how far you've come and how far you have to go.

Here's what employers have to say about education:

From Massachusetts:

"I wish that I could impress upon all young people in the first or second year of high school the value of an education and the value of appying themselves for what the future holds for them."

From New Jersey:

"Teenagers should aspire to gain as much formal edution as they desire and can afford. From existing reports and surveys, workers with the well-rounded education should be the most in demand in the future."

From Michigan:

"Education is the key to success in today's world. Perhaps the diploma has been overemphasized as a credential for employment—but what the diploma is presumed to represent cannot be overemphasized. Teenagers who don't plan to attend college should decide on a business or trade."

From New York:

"Every young person must decide what field seems best suited to him, then make every effort to learn as much as possible about it. For those capable of acquiring sound college training, the more the better. For those not suited for college training, a trade or vocational training is in order."

From California:

"A maximum of education is vitally essential, as most well-paying careers require an educated and well-trained person."

Girls should be aware that school is no longer merely a place to put in time till you meet the boy of your choice and decide to marry. As Dr. Evelyn G. Pitcher, of the Eliot-Pearson School, Tufts University, has said in discussing education for girls, "The female is reaching for education and growth as never before. Women will thereby have new worlds to conquer in politics, education, law, and medicine, as well as new gifts to bring to their careers as mothers and wives."

For girls who want the inside of their heads as up-to-date as the hair-do on the outside, there's no time like the high school years to absorb as much education as possible, get practical training in a skill from which they can make a living should the need arise, and pursue a vocation as one of their most important goals.

HOW TO MAKE HIGH SCHOOL COUNT

Ticket No. 1

Go to school with a purpose and plan to work

As a student, the main purpose of your life is to learn, and the only real way to learn is to work as hard as you can! In the long run, going to school just to get a diploma, and drifting instead of doing, won't give you much to go on. In fact, to get the best possible education today many educators advocate working outside class just as much as you work in it. If a class is forty minutes long, for example, you need approximately another forty minutes a day to study for the same subject.

Ticket No. 2

Maintain a good
high school record

When you plan to work and do your best, chances are that you'll maintain a reasonably good record—one that you can be proud of when other people see it.

Maintaining this record is important, too, since employers and schools may ask for your record before deciding whether or not you're for them. More often than not they'll want to check on your performance so far.

The so-so grade that you blame on the teacher or the just-passing mark that isn't your best won't be good enough! If that kind of work is an old habit of yours, get out of the rut at once by seeking the help of your guidance counselor and discussing your future with him. To the best of his ability he'll help you find ways to make better use of your time and get better grades.

Ticket No. 3

Keep your eye on
a general job field
or career goal

The need to have some sense of direction for your future career during the time you're in high school can't be overemphasized. As we've said before, when you have a sense of direction you can plan intelligently and test your abilities as you go. You can also read pertinent material, and try to get part-time, summer, or volunteer jobs in the right general area.

However, the average person will find it to his advantage to keep his eye on a general goal instead of on one specific job in a field.

For instance, if you're interested in music you don't have to determine now whether your best future opportunities will be in teaching, performing, or directing—just to mention three out of many opportunities. Instead, avail yourself of every opportunity to do everything possible in music.

When you plan things this way, you take the courses and do the things that give you a broad general education and keep the door open to more than one occupation in your chosen field—or even in another field, if necessary.

Ticket No. 4

Involve yourself in
extracurricular activities

Next to academic achievement, participation in extracurricular activities is your most important pursuit in high school. It will help you to become a many-sided person and view life through many windows. You'll learn. You'll have fun. And you'll develop that wonderful sense of belonging and being part of a group. You don't have to be a performer or the top student in the school to be important in extracurricular work, either.

One high school boy who wanted to be part of the school's dramatic activities and who wasn't in line to be the star on the stage became the star stagehand instead. As a result, he contributed so much to the school's dramatic and musical performances that he received a special award at graduation. Even after graduation, he occasionally came back to help backstage because he just seemed to "belong."

Naturally it's a wise step, in involving yourself in extracurricular activities, to pick ones that will do the most for your future. And do pick only as many as you can handle.

Doing well in your school work and contributing to two or three activities that mean something to you will count more than a huge listing under your name in the year book!

As for your choice of activities, participate in sports if you possibly can. This teaches you team work and getting along with others. Seek clubs that follow your interests. If you hope to be a lawyer, clergyman, politician, or business leader, take part in debates and participate in all available speaking opportunities. If music is your future, do extracurricular work in that.

Three young people who enjoyed singing together attended a pop show at their junior high school, heard a similar group sing, and asked, "Couldn't we?"

As a result, they formed their own trio and participated in many events all through high school. They also cut demonstration records and fulfilled a few professional engagements with established performers. All of them, as a result of this experience, continued their music education after high school.

Ticket No. 5

Stay in school until
you finish

One of the most familiar—as well as unhappy—words in the high school vocabulary today is the dismal and dreary word "dropout." The United States Office of Education estimates that 7,500,000 students will leave high school before graduation in the next decade. There are few decisions that spoil a young person's future career chances quite so effectually as dropping out. Every statistic bears this out. And observation bears out the statistics.

One girl who dropped out of school at sixteen answered the question "What advice would you give someone thinking of leaving school?" in these words:

"My life history is a picture that should turn anyone from even thinking of quitting school."

An unshaven, discouraged-looking man who came to the author's door one day to pick up papers for a welfare agency looked at her typewriter and asked what she did.

"You're lucky," he told her when she explained. "I quit the books in high school and I've never had a decent job."

A young woman wrote for advice in this vein:

Dear Roberta Roesch:

I'm a young mother without any skills. I also lack a high school diploma because I quit school and had a baby when I was seventeen. At the present time I have to find something to do, though, because we can no longer get along on my husband's pay. But he can't do any better because he quit high school, too.

Right now our bills are snowing us under, ruining his health, and making both of us feel that our youth is passing us by. I can't find a job, however, for the hours in which I can work when my husband is home to take care of the babies, and any work I can find for other hours doesn't pay me enough to leave us any profit after I pay a sitter.

Please help us get out of this box.

There's no simple answer, unfortunately, to situations like this, where foresight would have been better than the hindsight that came too late! The way to avoid this in your life is to follow the "stay in school" signs and postpone the many temptations that could lure you away.

Is There a Future When You've Dropped Out?

There's always a way to pull yourself up, regardless of how low you've dropped! So if you are a dropout and need help, or if you have friends who need help, your school principal, state employment office, minister, priest, or rabbi can direct you to the nearest job agency for youth in your area.

Other leads are the Neighborhood Youth Corps and the Job Corps.

The Neighborhood Youth Corps, as you probably know, is a youth work-training program that aids in the improvement of the education and skills of young people. Its purpose is to provide them with a new sense of direction and greater motivation by giving them an opportunity to serve the community and earn while they learn. You can obtain more information on the Youth Corps by inquiring at your local state employment service or talking to your local high school counseling office.

The Job Corps, whose motto is "Be somebody," is for young people sixteen through twenty-one years old who are out of school and who can't find a job or get into the armed forces. When you're accepted in this corps you live in a Job Corps center with other young people and receive added education, vocational training, and work experience. You learn how to get and hold a job, and you get paid for your period of service. To get further information on the Job Corps you can write to Job Corps, Office of Economic Opportunity, Washington, D.C. 20212.

Now that you have five tickets for making high school count, you can take the following test to see how well you're doing. This quiz will give you a good idea of your success in high school. On a separate piece of paper, or in your notebook, jot down your answers, yes or no.

"SEE YOURSELF" QUIZ

FOR EVALUATING YOUR SUCCESS SO FAR

1. Am I working as hard as I can?
2. Is my educational record good so far?
3. Am I in the upper half of my class?
4. Am I attending school with a purpose?
5. Do I participate in extracurricular activities?
6. Am I a good school citizen?
7. Do I know how to study?
8. Do I make good use of my time?
9. Do I show sufficient progress in my work?
10. Am I interested in my work?
11. Do I get along well with teachers and other students?
12. Do I have a fairly good idea of my plans for after high school?
13. Have I taken definite steps to find out what I need to do now to be ready for my future plans?
14. Do I know how to read quickly and can I comprehend accurately the main ideas in what I read?
15. Do I practice writing and speaking well?
16. Do I get my work in on time instead of falling behind?
17. Do I follow instructions and take orders agreeably?
18. Would my teachers and advisors rate me as being dependable and responsible?
19. Do I show initiative instead of leaning on people?
20. Do I take advantage of all the opportunities available to me in high school?

After you finish the tests, note the statements you answered with a "No." Then make concrete plans to improve yourself there.

8

The Right Course for You

YOUR best preparation for the future in choosing your high school course is a broad educational background. Such a base allows you a greater choice of jobs. And that kind of preparation will be necessary in your generation, as Peter F. Drucker, eminent management consultant, author and educator, wrote in *The Landmarks of Tomorrow.* "Since we live in an age of innovation, a practical education must prepare a man for work that does not yet exist and cannot yet be clearly defined. He must acquire basic tools of analysis, of expression, of understanding."

Generally speaking, the course that's right for you should be based upon (1) your "See Yourself" tests and analysis of yourself, (2) your school's analysis and record of you, and (3) the subjects you'll need to take for the future you plan.

Science Research Associates, one of the best sources of educational information in the country, lists in its publication "My Educational Plans," by Harold L. Munson, the high school courses listed below. You're probably taking one of them—or deciding on one—right now, but there's no time like the present for being sure you're right.

1. *Academic or college preparatory program.* This program is designed to prepare students for entrance into college. The subjects usually included in such a program are English, social studies, science, mathematics and languages. In such a program there is not as wide a choice of electives as in others. Students are expected to work hard in order to complete the basic requirements.

2. *Technical program.* This program offers a basic foundation in mathematics and science. It provides additional technical training in such subjects as drafting, machine shop theory, design, and others. A technical program offers good preparation for entrance into an engineering college or technical institute. It is also excellent preparation for apprenticeship and industrial training programs.

However, you should be aware of the fact that a technical program is extremely specialized. Once you embark upon such a course, it is difficult to make later changes.

3. *Vocational program.* This program is designed to prepare you for work in a skilled trade after high school. If you carry the required academic work in addition to the vocational subjects, this program can also prepare you for entrance into junior colleges, trade schools, technical institutes, and agricultural schools. However, it is wise to consult college catalogues and to discuss your goals with your counselor if you want to take a vocational program and still attend college. If you are planning to become a skilled tradesman (auto mechanic, beautician, machinist, carpenter) you may find it advisable to plan for additional training in your trade after high school.

4. *Commercial program.* This program prepares young men and women for business occupations. Secretarial, stenographic, retailing, office practice, and general business courses are usually offered as part of the commercial program. Much of the training in this program, in subjects such as typing and shorthand, requires many hours of

practice. Although students are usually prepared to take jobs immediately after graduation, it is often desirable for them to take additional training in a business school. Some students may wish to take related programs in junior colleges or technical institutes.

If you select a commercial program, you should be aware of the fact that it is specialized, and you should be quite certain that you want a career in business.

5. *General program.* Many high schools offer a general program designed to give broad rather than specialized or college-preparatory training. In addition to the courses required for graduation, students in a general program may choose subjects that best relate to their interests, aptitudes, and abilities. Such programs require careful planning, with help from your counselor, teacher, and parents.

Generally speaking, if there's any chance at all that you may go to college, hang on to the college preparatory, or academic, course if you possibly can. Then you'll have the right course if you need it. If you don't need it, you can always get vocational education later and still have a good basic education behind you.

On the other hand, if all signposts—including your special interests—point to the fact that the academic life is not for you, a technical or vocational high school course is a practical choice.

Keep your eye on the type of job you want. That will determine to a great extent the courses you'll need to take and the amount of education you'll need as preparation.

Here's a brief rundown of jobs available at different educational levels:

Less than four years of high school: factory worker, food store worker, laundry helper, truck driver, bus boy, waitress, parking lot attendant, gas station attendant, sales clerk, farm worker.

Graduation from a general or commercial high school course: Office clerk, civil service worker, telephone operator, salesman, saleswoman, photographer, typist, library attendant, stenographer, file clerk, bookkeeper, receptionist.

Graduation from vocational high school course: auto mechanic, beauty-service operator, practical nurse, baker, cook, welder, apprentice in such trades as printing and carpentry, cabinetmaker, butcher, appliance serviceman.

One to three years' training beyond high school: medical or dental assistant, technician, technologist, draftsman, hospital-trained nurse, data processor, programmer, executive secretary, illustrator, commercial artist, model, store manager, office supervisor.

Four or more years beyond high school: librarian, lawyer, physician, dentist, pharmacist, teacher, chemist, biologist, psychologist, educational administrator, engineer, social worker, home economist.

Most of the time the special aptitude, vocational, I.Q., personal and social adjustment, and achievement tests available to you in high school can help you choose your course.

They can show you your strong points and weak points, reveal your interests and point up your abilities. Even more important, they can follow up an interest test with an aptitude test to see whether you have the aptitude to pursue that interest vocationally.

A school testing program can be a valuable guide to the right course when tests are used to measure you and evaluate you in connection with everything else.

They're not valuable, however, when you get mixed up with a test-happy administrator like the one who put so much stock in tests that he insisted upon changing the classes of a student who was working hard and doing adequately in her class but whose latest I.Q. test indicated that her I.Q. was too low for the class she was in.

"But she's doing as well as anyone else," said the teacher, who went to bat for her. "Her performance is up to par!"

"It doesn't matter about her performance!" insisted the test-happy administrator. "Her work on the test is the guide."

If that sorry fate is ever yours and you find yourself in a spot where a piece of paper counts more than a human being, get your whole family up to bat and descend upon the school. No one intended testing to be used like that!

On the whole, the best approach to any testing program is (1) do as well as you can on the tests, (2) use them as one measuring stick for your future plans and courses, and (3) add to test results your own will, determination, performance, and confidence in yourself.

Special Educational Opportunities Offered in Cooperation with Local Businesses

1. *"Distributive Education"*

Essentially, distributive education is a vocational phase of the business education program. A distributive occupation is defined as one followed by proprietors, managers, or employees engaged primarily in marketing or merchandising goods or services. In a distributive education course high school students sixteen years of age or older study marketing, merchandising, and selling while working on a part-time basis in stores and other distributive occupations. The student is paid for the hours he works. Under such a program you might sell in food stores, variety stores, service stations, drugstores, hardware stores, appliance stores, furniture stores, shoe stores, florist shops, or restaurants.

Let's take the case of William Neely as an example of how such programs operate. Under a distributive education program Neely went to work in high school as a student learner in a grocery store for one of the country's grocery store chains. Following his graduation he remained at his training station for three years to become produce manager. Later he moved up to other managerial posts, and eventually won an assignment as manager of one of the Jewel Food Stores' top establishments.

2. *Cooperative Education*

Cooperative education is a program for high school students at least sixteen years old who wish to attend school and also hold part-time paid and supervised positions in offices. In a cooperative education course a student might address envelopes in a utility firm, work in a mail room, or type in a bank, to mention only three examples.

When Anne Pucciariello went to high school under this program, she worked half a day at the Schering Corporation during the second half of her Senior year. As a result, she received ten credits for graduation, an award in her school assembly as the Senior considered by the business department faculty the one most likely to succeed in commercial activities, and a full-time job at Schering after her graduation.

Selection for such programs is usually based on scholastic achievement, attendance, punctuality, appearance, future career choice, and recommendation by teachers and counselors.

If you're interested in looking into either type of education, ask your guidance counselor about the availability of these programs in your school.

No matter what high school course you choose, be flexible. Learn to look forward to other educational experiences and opportunities. Learn as early in life as possible how to adapt yourself and your plans to a world that changes constantly.

A booklet appropriately called "Adjusting to Change" quotes a prominent commencement speaker as saying to young people on the move, "If there were some kind of training course that young people could take to prepare themselves for their future, I would suggest a course that would help them to be always adaptable to change. Being adaptable is fundamental to success. In such a training course, they would learn that they cannot be successful for very long without adopting new ideas. The successful person not only learns to be flexible to new ideas and new approaches, but he learns to look for them as well."

9

Choose a Job Field Where You Can Succeed

IF you're a boy (and possibly if you're a girl) you'll spend a good forty years of your life working and earning a living.

Chances are great that your job will be your life story,

so the best approach to plotting it successfully is to map out a general outline. You can't predict the entire plan of your future; the world of jobs is a changing world these days. But you can go forward to meet tomorrow by making your tentative plans today.

Ticket No. 1

Learn as much as possible
about the major occupational fields
and the main jobs within each field

Start now haunting your school or town library for books, pamphlets and trade publications in the career fields that interest you most. This will be a first step. It will also prepare you to delve into more of the sources of information you'll find in the "Suggested Reading List" and "Sources for Further Information" at the end of this book. You'll also find other sources listed in Chapter X.

Ticket No. 2

Learn what job fields
are expected to grow

Aim at a job field that is secure or expected to grow.

Generally speaking, employment experts predict that scientific and technological fields, clerical work, and sales and service occupations will all grow. No increase, however, is expected for laborers. A further decrease is expected for farm workers.

Health services are expected to expand. Many more doctors and nurses will be needed. The entire field of dentistry—with its openings for dentists, dental hygienists and technicians—will offer much opportunity, since presently there are barely enough practicing dentists to care for half of the population. There will be a great need for social workers, engineers, chemists, physicists, mathematicians, lawyers, and insurance and banking employees.

Teachers are needed for almost every branch of education. Librarians are a special need, too.

Job opportunities will run high in religion, home economics, occupational therapy, dietetics, and programing. Skilled machinists, machine tool operators, toolmakers, diesinkers and setters, skilled craftsmen, and various kinds of mechanics and repairmen will all be needed.

To keep up with the growth in job fields while you're deciding on your future, studying ads in newspapers will give you a good idea of the prospects for employment in various fields. The change in the number of workers in a job field is a good indicator of employment possibilities.

Ticket No. 3

As you study job fields, determine
as well as you can which ones
fit you and your needs

The best way to do this is to take the following "See Yourself" test for each job field that interests you. Write the answers in your "See Yourself" notebook:

"SEE YOURSELF" JOB FIELD TEST

1. What are my present strengths and weaknesses for this field of work?
2. What are my special aptitudes for it?
3. What personal traits have I that would be helpful in it?
4. What concrete examples of my interest in the field can I show to date?
5. What qualifications have I for it so far?
6. What education and training will I need to enter this field?

7. What are my financial resources for getting this? Or how can I obtain the necessary financial resources?
8. What work experience—if any—have I had in this field in part-time, summer, or volunteer jobs? If I've had experience, how did I like it?
9. Have I the physical and mental capacity necessary to work in this field?
10. How well does it fit the goals I have in mind?
11. What are the chances for advancement in it?
12. What is the salary range? Will it provide the life I'd like to have and the needs I'd like filled? At the same time will it give me inner satisfaction and contentment?
13. Where will I find work in this field when I'm ready to enter it?
14. What will the working conditions be?
15. Is the employment outlook good?
16. What jobs will be available in the job field and what am I likely to do in each one?

Ticket No. 4

*Decide which of your interests
or talents is likely to provide
you with your best chance*

When Walt Disney was deciding on his future he had two ambitions pulling at him for career choices.

On one hand, he'd sketched and drawn as far back as he could remember and even sold some "drawings" when he was seven to a retired doctor. In high school he studied drawing, did illustrations for the school paper, and went to night school to learn cartooning.

On the other hand, Walt was also interested in the theater, and during his growing up years he won prizes for his impersonations. Consequently, when it was time—after World War I and a series of miscellaneous jobs—to get down to the serious business of choosing a career,

Disney took stock of himself. Should he be an actor or an artist?

It would be easier, he decided, to get a job as an artist. So an artist he would be!

His first art job was with an advertising company in Kansas City that did work for farm journals. Here he was required to draw such things as egg-laying mash, salt blocks for cattle and other farm equipment. And, since he was merely an apprentice, the two other artists in the company kept him turning out rough sketches, which they finished themselves, often changing them entirely!

Ticket No. 5

Keep your job goals 90% realistic!
But at the same time throw in 10% of faith
and hope, because sometimes it's that
10% of faith and hope that wins.

Your own interests and abilities, along with your "See Yourself" tests, will help you to be realistic and show you how futile it is to try to be a singer if you can't sing, or a baseball player if you can't bat a ball! Concentrate on the fields and the jobs where the odds will be for you rather than against you.

Ticket No. 6

Avoid the trap of picking a job field
because it looks glamorous on the
outside. Look on the inside, too.

The glamour in many job fields is like the glittering, shining wrapping on a Christmas package or the frothy bubbles on top of your soda. It's the part that most people see, but there is more to a job than the glitter and froth.

Many people, for instance, picture writers' lives as a wonderful package of glamour. But they seldom see the endless work—which a real writer has to love—behind every autograph party. If they chose the glamour without loving the work, the glitter would soon be gone.

Ticket No. 7

*Similarly, avoid the trap of
picking a job field solely
for the money you'll earn*

Certainly, making money is a part of every job. But a job is also a way of life and an interest that takes you through life, and if it doesn't give you happiness along with cash, you'll end up never getting paid in contentment and satisfaction. Often, though, when a job pays in pleasure it also pays in profit.

Henry Ford, who earned his share of both pleasure and profit, summed it up when he said, "I have always believed that if you go into a career for money and nothing but money, you will not get it. But if you go into a career sincerely and well-prepared to do something useful, you'll never lack the money to carry it out."

Ticket No. 8

*Look for a job that will
serve some purpose and be useful,
and never measure it by "status"*

By the right standards, there's no such thing as a low-status job or a high-status job if the work serves the needs of the world and if the person who does it wants to do it, likes to do it, feels useful doing it and does it well.

Ticket No. 9

*If you're a girl, keep your views
of the future down-to-earth instead
of up-in-the-clouds*

Rosy pink clouds are part of life and it's right to be on them sometimes while you cherish the very feminine dream of marriage, family, and home. Womanhood is at its best when these rosy dreams come true, but today marriage is not often a woman's whole life.

Prophecies for girls and their futures indicate that eight out of ten women will work a good many years of their lives. A twenty-year-old girl, if she remains single, will spend some forty years in the labor market. If, after working a few years, a girl marries, has a family and then goes back to work at thirty, she's still likely to work for some twenty-three more years.

The United States Department of Labor, in a bulletin called "Choosing A Career," reprinted from the "Occupational Outlook Handbook," puts it this way:

"Based on studies by the Bureau of Labor Statistics, most girls can expect the following life pattern as they move from school to middle and old age. Most unmarried girls will go to work at age seventeen or eighteen (unless they go to college). Within three or four years, most of these girls will marry. Some of them will then stop working for pay in order to get a new home organized, but a majority will continue to work, either to help put a husband through school, to supplement a husband's income, or to permit purchase of a home, a car, or labor-saving equipment. Then, when the first baby arrives, the vast majority of young mothers give up their jobs and remain out of the labor market until their youngest child is old enough to go to school. It is true that as many as one in five women with preschool-age children do continue to work, usually because of economic necessity, but the general pattern is that the age group twenty-five to thirty-four supplies the lowest proportion of women workers.

"When the youngest child no longer needs constant care, the trek of mothers back to paid employment begins. This usually happens when the women are approaching their middle thirties, after they have been non-wage earners for about eight to ten years. Once back, the tendency is for them to remain in the labor force, perhaps not continuously, but certainly for a substantial proportion of their years to age sixty-five. By 1975, nearly half of all women between thirty-five and sixty-five will probably be either working or looking for work. Unless things change radically and unexpectedly in the years ahead, the highest participation rate will be among women age forty-five to fifty-four.

"These comments have concentrated on the life pattern of married women because these women will be in the vast majority. But for the girl who remains single—and one in ten does—the length of her working life will be little different from that of a man. Since most single women must support themselves, and often parents or other relatives, they must continue to hold a job. The "work-life expectancy," as it is often referred to, looks like this for women: For single women, forty years at work; for childless married women, about thirty years; and for married women with children, somewhat less. Girls, then, may well give serious thought to the kind of work they want to do and can do best."

With everything pointing to this down-to-earth fact, it's wise to consider a job field—if you have the aptitude for one—that you can keep up, or work in on a part-time basis (should you need to or choose to) during the years you may stay at home while your children are young. Excellent choices for this are teaching, music, secretarial work, writing, home economics, art, interior design, and other fields with free-lance opportunities.

Ticket No. 10

*Discuss your career choice with
school counselors, teachers, and people
who work in the field*

Much of the time the advice you get will be excellent. But at the same time you weigh everyone else's suggestions you must also have a little confidence in your own potential—provided that you're willing to pay in time and effort the price you must pay to develop that potential.

One high school boy, whose career choice was engineering above all else, failed in a competitive mathematics test he took for entrance to the school he hoped to attend. Because of his failure he was advised to forget engineering and turn to something else.

Happily, though, his ten per cent of hope, which we have mentioned in a previous ticket, came to his rescue. He kept looking for schools until he found one that enrolled him in the aeronautical engineering course. The first year, however, he failed in mathematics and had to repeat the subject that summer.

Even with the summer work, things didn't go well his second year. Then the college suggested that he drop out of school, since it was obvious he wasn't geared for his career choice. By that time his parents were saying the same thing.

Now, though, the financial situation said No, so the only way the boy could stay in college and take advantage of his improved grades was to get a daytime job and attend college at night. For a year he used this system, and he dropped a year behind his class. But later he was able to return to daytime classes, and ultimately he received his aeronautical engineering degree.

His first job was with an aircraft company, and he did so well that when the aircraft company's contracts were

canceled six months after he started working he was
offered a job with the United States Navy.

Within his first five years of working in this job field he'd
been told to forget, the young man was promoted to the
post of project engineer in charge of the operation of a
very valuable wind tunnel for testing new designs in air-
crafts and missiles—an exceptional promotion for his
age.

As a result of his work he also received a "Superior
Achievement Award," only the second one of its kind
presented at that time for continuing outstanding work in
the redesign and successful testing of advanced principles
in missile conformation.

Ironically, all the work this young man did to achieve
such success was based—along with determination, dili-
gence, and faith—on mathematics far beyond anything
he'd failed in school!

Ticket No. 11

*Whenever possible get the feel of a
vocational field by joining a
"Future" club*

Today the "Future" clubs, which began with Future
Homemakers, Future Farmers, and Future Teachers, are
expanding into many other professions. Presently there
are clubs for future physicians, nurses, physicists, chemists, geologists, meteorologists, and psychologists. When
you belong to one of them you gain valuable views of
these professions from speakers, field trips, and on-the-job
experience in either a volunteer or paid basis.

Future nurses, for example, deliver trays, fill water
pitchers, run errands, and do other hospital chores. Future physicians learn how to measure blood pressure, listen to medical lectures, and tour hospitals. Future teach-

ers help out with an occasional class while the regular teacher lends a hand, too.

All of this is helpful, according to accounts from members of the clubs reported by Phyllis W. Goldman in an article in *The New York Times Magazine.*

One high school Junior who was considering teaching joined a club and assisted elementary school teachers several afternoons doing such things as helping with reading, making costumes for plays, coaching children in their parts, and giving suggestions on how to put puzzles together.

"You can read a lot in books," this girl said. "But you have to actually do the work to really learn about it. By learning about it this way I found that I love little kids and that elementary education is my real calling."

A boy who wanted to be a doctor and who joined the Future Physicians Club summed up his "feel" of a vocational field this way:

"At a medical convention I watched a delicate internal examination being performed on an elderly man. At first it disgusted me, but then I began to realize that if you want to help people you have to get used to that sort of thing."

Ticket No. 12

Beat automation by preparing for it

The machines in automation's kingdom can never be as important as people, because machines aren't human!

Max Hess, a retailer who employs a good many young people, said, "We can't foresee automation taking the place of personal service. There will continue to be a need for that personal service."

Other employers feel the same when it comes to young people's futures.

The way to beat automation at its own game is to prepare yourself to give the personal service and do the work that automation can't do. When you safeguard your future this way, automation can be a help instead of a hindrance, because the technological changes it provides also provide new kinds of jobs, greater productivity in these jobs and an age of miracles and marvels.

Ticket No. 13

Consider professional guidance if you
can't get off the ground in career choosing

Of course, you'll have to make your own vocational decision in the end. But when you've made no start at all toward that decision it's possible some sound vocational guidance will help you pinpoint your interests. If you do decide on vocational counseling, try your school guidance office first.

The school can check on the qualifications of a counseling agency. It can also find out whether the service is listed in the "Directory of Approved Counseling Services" put out by the American Personnel and Guidance Association. Not all the good agencies are included in this directory, but all of the agencies listed are considered reliable. Fees for vocational guidance and testing vary. They can start at approximately $35 and go up to over $100.

Sometimes free vocational counseling is yours for the asking from organizations right in your own community. One source, for instance, is the United States Employment Service. Other sources are churches, YMCA's, the Boys' Clubs of America, and 4-H Clubs. Inquire about these sources in your community.

If you seek vocational counseling take with you all the information you've learned about yourself from your "See Yourself" tests and other sources. By doing this, you'll be able to give your vocational counselor a better picture of your problems and background from your viewpoint. You'll also be better prepared to fill out questionnaires about your education, experience, hobbies, interests, aims, likes and dislikes. Aptitude and vocational tests may also be part of the counseling. As your counselor talks to you and tests you he will try to show you how to match your background, experience, and aptitudes to the needs of the job world.

Ticket No. 14

Build into all your job plans the ability to be flexible

We began this chapter on choosing job fields by pointing out the fact that the job world is a changing world these days. Just as you need to be flexible to get the most out of your education, you will need to be flexible to get the most out of your job choice. Always, you'll have to change with change to get the most from your future!

As W. Willard Wirtz, United States Secretary of Labor, has pointed out, "Tomorrow belongs to those who face change honestly, squarely, eagerly . . . who go forward to meet it . . . who see change as an essential quality of growth, who see growth as the meaning of life, and who believe that the future is a good idea."

10

A Full View of Your Job Field

An 1870 statistic listed approximately 338 vocations. Today, the United States Employment Service lists more than 22,000 different jobs with over 40,000 job titles.

To spotlight each job would take volumes instead of a single chapter, so this chapter will spotlight the ten job fields revealed to be most popular by a recent survey.

Each job tree in the following section represents one field of work, and each branch represents one job in that field. Naturally, all the branches of each field cannot be shown. There are far too many jobs. So think of the ones you see hanging here as only a sampling of all the jobs available.

If you would like to learn about more possible jobs in one area, write to the source listed at the base of each tree. These organizations can also furnish specific information such as what you would do in each job, qualifications needed, where you would find work, how and where you would train, and the salary range.

These job trees are only a view in passing of the whole vocational forest that you can explore on your own.

In addition to the "Suggested Reading List" and the "Sources of Further Information" at the back of this book,

MEDICINE AND HEALTH SERVICES

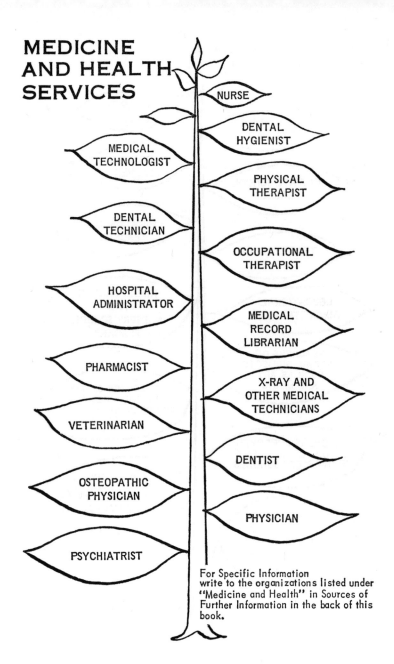

NURSE

DENTAL HYGIENIST

MEDICAL TECHNOLOGIST

PHYSICAL THERAPIST

DENTAL TECHNICIAN

OCCUPATIONAL THERAPIST

HOSPITAL ADMINISTRATOR

MEDICAL RECORD LIBRARIAN

PHARMACIST

X-RAY AND OTHER MEDICAL TECHNICIANS

VETERINARIAN

DENTIST

OSTEOPATHIC PHYSICIAN

PHYSICIAN

PSYCHIATRIST

For Specific Information
write to the organizations listed under
"Medicine and Health" in Sources of
Further Information in the back of this
book.

TEACHING AND EDUCATION

PRIMARY TEACHER

ELEMENTARY TEACHER

JUNIOR HIGH TEACHER

PRIVATE SCHOOL TEACHER

HIGH SCHOOL TEACHER

TRADE SCHOOL TEACHER

EDUCATIONAL ADMINISTRATORS

KINDERGARTEN AND NURSERY SCHOOL TEACHER

TEACHERS OF SPECIAL SUBJECTS SUCH AS ART AND MUSIC

TEACHERS OF THE HANDICAPPED AND CHILDREN WITH SPECIAL PROBLEMS

TEACHERS EMPLOYED BY U.S. GOVERNMENT IN OVERSEAS SCHOOLS

CONSULTING PSYCHOLOGISTS AND TEACHERS OF THE SOCIALLY MALADJUSTED

COLLEGE AND UNIVERSITY INSTRUCTORS & PROFESSORS

Write to
National Educational Association
Research Division
1201 16th St., N. W.
Washington, D. C. 20036

ENGINEERING

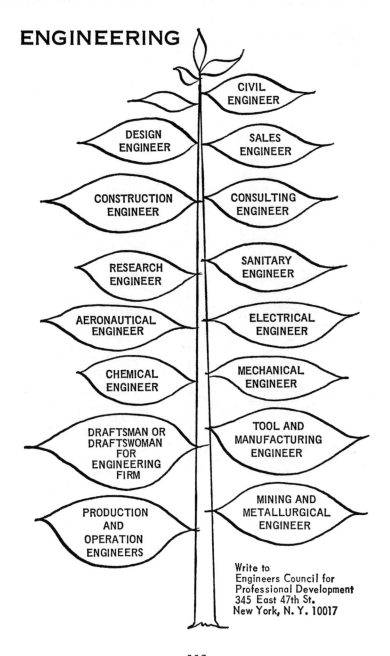

CIVIL ENGINEER

DESIGN ENGINEER

SALES ENGINEER

CONSTRUCTION ENGINEER

CONSULTING ENGINEER

RESEARCH ENGINEER

SANITARY ENGINEER

AERONAUTICAL ENGINEER

ELECTRICAL ENGINEER

CHEMICAL ENGINEER

MECHANICAL ENGINEER

DRAFTSMAN OR DRAFTSWOMAN FOR ENGINEERING FIRM

TOOL AND MANUFACTURING ENGINEER

PRODUCTION AND OPERATION ENGINEERS

MINING AND METALLURGICAL ENGINEER

Write to
Engineers Council for
Professional Development
345 East 47th St.
New York, N. Y. 10017

HOME ECONOMICS

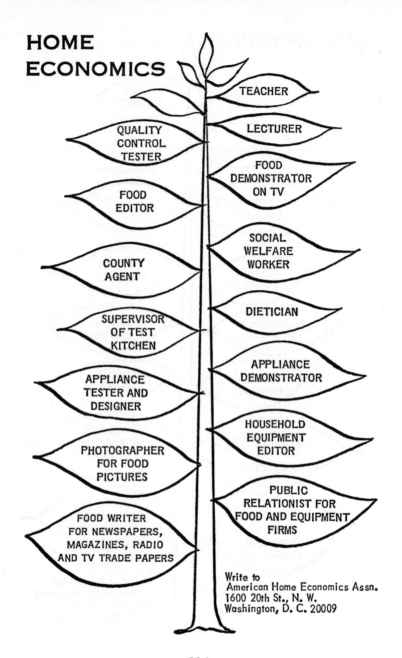

TEACHER

LECTURER

QUALITY CONTROL TESTER

FOOD DEMONSTRATOR ON TV

FOOD EDITOR

SOCIAL WELFARE WORKER

COUNTY AGENT

DIETICIAN

SUPERVISOR OF TEST KITCHEN

APPLIANCE DEMONSTRATOR

APPLIANCE TESTER AND DESIGNER

HOUSEHOLD EQUIPMENT EDITOR

PHOTOGRAPHER FOR FOOD PICTURES

PUBLIC RELATIONIST FOR FOOD AND EQUIPMENT FIRMS

FOOD WRITER FOR NEWSPAPERS, MAGAZINES, RADIO AND TV TRADE PAPERS

Write to
American Home Economics Assn.
1600 20th St., N. W.
Washington, D. C. 20009

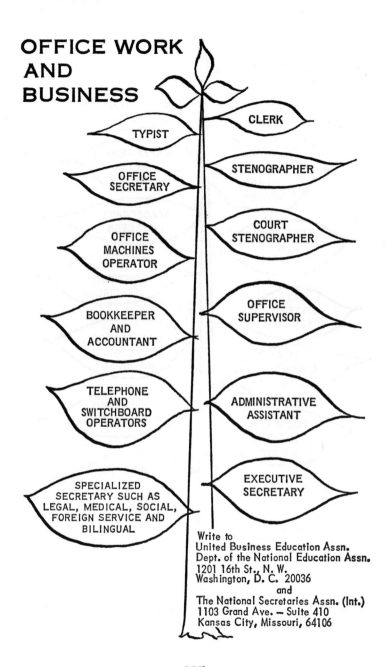

OFFICE WORK
AND
BUSINESS

CLERK

TYPIST

STENOGRAPHER

OFFICE
SECRETARY

COURT
STENOGRAPHER

OFFICE
MACHINES
OPERATOR

OFFICE
SUPERVISOR

BOOKKEEPER
AND
ACCOUNTANT

TELEPHONE
AND
SWITCHBOARD
OPERATORS

ADMINISTRATIVE
ASSISTANT

SPECIALIZED
SECRETARY SUCH AS
LEGAL, MEDICAL, SOCIAL,
FOREIGN SERVICE AND
BILINGUAL

EXECUTIVE
SECRETARY

Write to
United Business Education Assn.
Dept. of the National Education Assn.
1201 16th St., N. W.
Washington, D. C. 20036
          and
The National Secretaries Assn. (Int.)
1103 Grand Ave. — Suite 410
Kansas City, Missouri, 64106

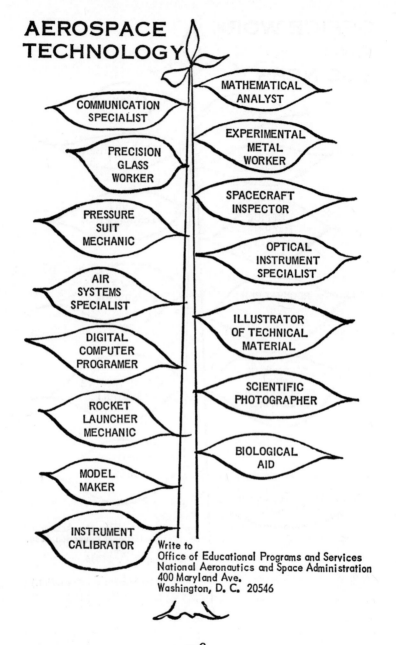

AEROSPACE TECHNOLOGY

COMMUNICATION SPECIALIST

MATHEMATICAL ANALYST

PRECISION GLASS WORKER

EXPERIMENTAL METAL WORKER

PRESSURE SUIT MECHANIC

SPACECRAFT INSPECTOR

AIR SYSTEMS SPECIALIST

OPTICAL INSTRUMENT SPECIALIST

DIGITAL COMPUTER PROGRAMER

ILLUSTRATOR OF TECHNICAL MATERIAL

ROCKET LAUNCHER MECHANIC

SCIENTIFIC PHOTOGRAPHER

MODEL MAKER

BIOLOGICAL AID

INSTRUMENT CALIBRATOR

Write to
Office of Educational Programs and Services
National Aeronautics and Space Administration
400 Maryland Ave.
Washington, D. C. 20546

MUSIC

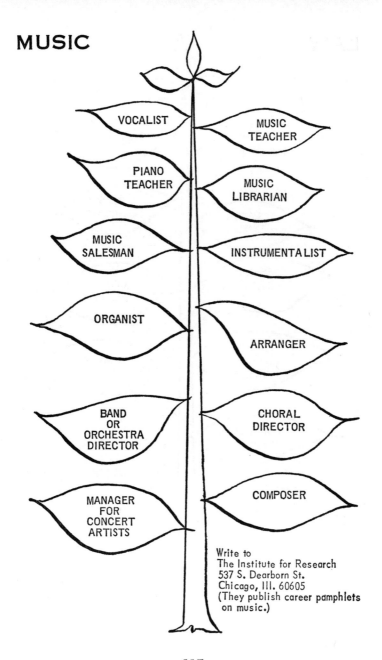

VOCALIST

MUSIC TEACHER

PIANO TEACHER

MUSIC LIBRARIAN

MUSIC SALESMAN

INSTRUMENTALIST

ORGANIST

ARRANGER

BAND OR ORCHESTRA DIRECTOR

CHORAL DIRECTOR

MANAGER FOR CONCERT ARTISTS

COMPOSER

Write to
The Institute for Research
537 S. Dearborn St.
Chicago, Ill. 60605
(They publish career pamphlets
on music.)

LAW

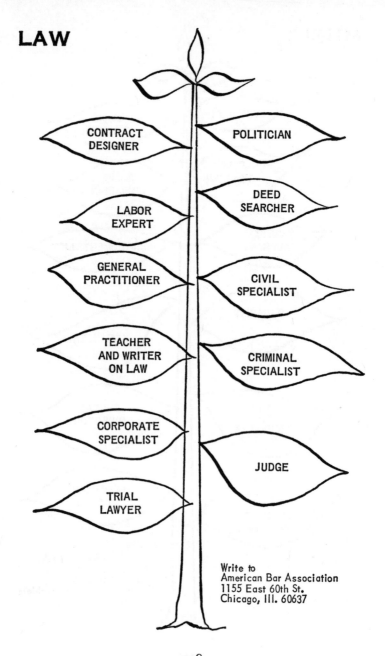

CONTRACT DESIGNER

POLITICIAN

LABOR EXPERT

DEED SEARCHER

GENERAL PRACTITIONER

CIVIL SPECIALIST

TEACHER AND WRITER ON LAW

CRIMINAL SPECIALIST

CORPORATE SPECIALIST

JUDGE

TRIAL LAWYER

Write to
American Bar Association
1155 East 60th St.
Chicago, Ill. 60637

118

SOCIAL WORK

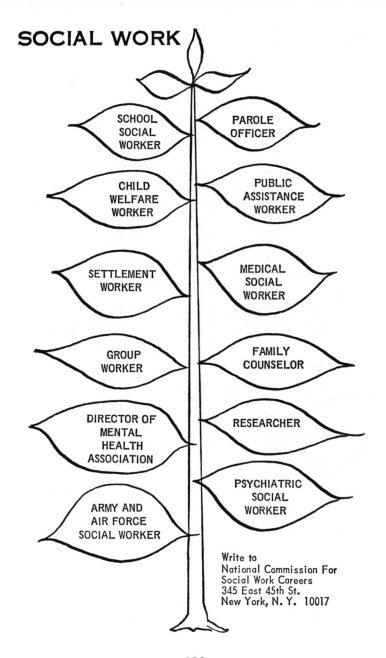

SCHOOL SOCIAL WORKER

PAROLE OFFICER

CHILD WELFARE WORKER

PUBLIC ASSISTANCE WORKER

SETTLEMENT WORKER

MEDICAL SOCIAL WORKER

GROUP WORKER

FAMILY COUNSELOR

DIRECTOR OF MENTAL HEALTH ASSOCIATION

RESEARCHER

ARMY AND AIR FORCE SOCIAL WORKER

PSYCHIATRIC SOCIAL WORKER

Write to
National Commission For
Social Work Careers
345 East 45th St.
New York, N. Y. 10017

SCIENCE

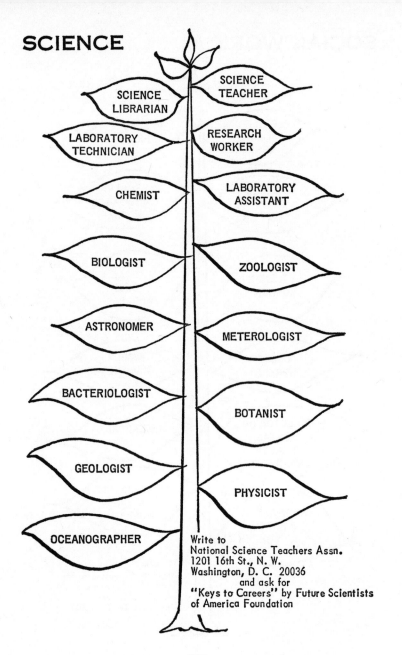

SCIENCE TEACHER

SCIENCE LIBRARIAN

RESEARCH WORKER

LABORATORY TECHNICIAN

CHEMIST

LABORATORY ASSISTANT

BIOLOGIST

ZOOLOGIST

ASTRONOMER

METEROLOGIST

BACTERIOLOGIST

BOTANIST

GEOLOGIST

PHYSICIST

OCEANOGRAPHER

Write to
National Science Teachers Assn.
1201 16th St., N. W.
Washington, D. C. 20036
and ask for
"Keys to Careers" by Future Scientists
of America Foundation

here are a few additional good sources of information. Check with your local library or your guidance counselor's office. You can probably refer to them there.

Career Opportunities:

A series of fifty-seven articles designed to help guide young people to a better future. Published in paperback by Career Information Service, New York Life Insurance Company, 51 Madison Avenue, New York, New York 10010. Available in school guidance offices and public libraries.

Career Preview:

A directory of jobs and careers. This pocket-size directory includes names and addresses of sources from which to get free or inexpensive literature. Especially prepared to introduce young people to a cross section of useful and rewarding careers. Published by Enterprise Publications, 20 N. Wacker Drive, Chicago, Illinois 60606. Available for 35¢.

Occupational Outlook Handbook:

This excellent source book describes some seven hundred occupations—nature of work, training and qualifications, income, working conditions, future outlook. Published by the Department of Labor and available from Superintendent of Documents, Government Printing Office, Washington, D.C. 20402. Price $4.75. (Your library will probably have it.) Supplements to this handbook publish up-to-the-minute information on new occupations.

Job Guide for Young Workers:

This seventy-two page booklet describes jobs that can be obtained after graduating from high school—duties and qualifications, qualifications for employ-

ment, and advancement prospects, and where the job
is to be found. Published by the Department of Labor
and available from Superintendent of Documents,
Government Printing Office, Washington, D.C.
20402. Price 45¢.

Job Guide for Young Workers in New York City:
Although this two-hundred-page book was prepared
for workers in New York City, it's a bible of information, as far as job descriptions go, for young high
school graduates seeking first jobs. There are separate
indexes for boys' jobs and girls' jobs and one index
for all jobs included in the *Guide*. In most cases, a
full page of pertinent information is given on each
job. Published by New York State Department of
Labor Division of Employment, 370 Seventh Avenue,
New York, New York 10001. Ask your school counselor if he has a copy.

The Wonderful World of Biography

Besides the kind of vocational literature listed above, another fine source of information, as well as inspiration, is
the great world of biography. In reading about the career
of an eminent person you'll get the "feel" of his job field in
one of the best ways of all.

What's Your Interest?

Art

Artist in Iowa: A Life of Grant Wood, by Darrell Gar-
wood

Dear Theo, the Autobiography, by Vincent Van Gogh,
edited by Irving Stone

Grandma Moses, My Life's History, by Anna Mary Moses,
edited by Otto Kallir

The Man Whistler, by Hesketh Pearson

Norman Rockwell, Illustrator, by Arthur Leighton Guptill

Renoir, My Father, by Jean Renoir, translated by Randolph and Dorothy Weaver

Science
Dr. George Washington Carver, Scientist, by Shirley Graham
The Life of Pasteur, by René Vallery-Radot
The Life of Sir Alexander Fleming: Discoverer of Penicillin, by André Maurois
Madame Curie, a Biography, by Eve Curie, translated by Vincent Sheean
Men Against Death, by Paul Henry DeKruif

Dancing
Flight of the Swan: A Memory of Anna Pavlova, by André Oliveroff
And Promenade Home, by Agnes DeMille

Business and Industry
Andrew Carnegie, Autobiography, by Andrew Carnegie
Baruch: My Own Story, by Bernard Mannes Baruch
Henry Ford: A Great Life in Brief, by Roger Burlingame
Life of an American Workman, by Walter P. Chrysler, in collaboration with Boyden Sparkes

Religion
Living of These Days, an autobiography, by Harry Emerson Fosdick
A Man Called Peter, by Catherine Marshall

Theater
Act One: An Autobiography, by Moss Hart
Curtain Going Up: The Story of Katharine Cornell, by Gladys Malvern
Maude Adams: An Intimate Portrait, by Phyllis Robbins
Me and Kit, by Guthrie McClintic
Memories: An Autobiography, by Ethel Barrymore
A Quite Remarkable Father, by Leslie Ruth Howard

We Barrymores, by Lionel Barrymore

Teaching and Education

Each One Teach One: Frank Laubach, Friend to Millions, by Marjorie Medary

A Goodly Fellowship, by Mary Ellen Chase

The Touch of Magic: The Story of Helen Keller's Great Teacher, Anne Sullivan Macy, by Lorena A. Hickok

Up From Slavery: An Autobiography, by Booker T. Washington

Exploring

Beyond Adventure: The Lives of Three Explorers, by Ray Chapman Andrews

Vagrant Viking: My Life and Adventures, by Peter Freuchen

Flying

Lonely Sky, by William Bridgeman and Jacqueline Hazard

Stars at Noon, by Jacqueline Cochran

Law

Clarence Darrow, Defense Attorney, by Iris Noble

Final Verdict, by Adela Rogers St. Johns

Music

Beloved Friend (The Story of Peter Ilyich Tschaikowsky), by Katherine Drinker Bowen and Madejda von Meck

A Family on Wheels, by Marie Augusta Trapp, with Ruth R. Murdock

Gershwin Years, by Edward Jablonski and Lawrence D. Stewart

Interrupted Melody: The Story of My Life, by Marjorie Lawrence

Leonard Bernstein: The Man, His Work, and His World, by John Briggs

My Lord, What a Morning, by Marian Anderson

The Story of Irving Berlin, by David Ewen
The Story of Jerome Kern, by David Ewen
Van Cliburn Legend, by Abram Chasins with Villa Stiles

Government and Public Life

Baruch: The Public Years, by Bernard M. Baruch
Profiles in Courage, by John F. Kennedy

Medicine

Arctic Doctor, by Joseph P. Moody, with W. deGroot van
    Embden
Dr. Schweitzer of Lambaréné, by Norman Cousins
Doctors Mayo, by Helen Bernice Clapesattle
Memoirs of Childhood and Youth, by Albert Schweitzer
My Hospital in the Hills, by Gordon Stifler Seagrave
Promises to Keep: The Life of Doctor Thomas A. Dooley,
    by Agnes W. Dooley
Three Worlds of Albert Schweitzer, by Robert Payne

Writing and Journalism

A Peculiar Treasure, by Edna Ferber
Always the Young Strangers, by Carl Sandburg
Anatomy of Me: A Wonderer in Search of Herself, by
    Fannie Hurst
I Wanted To Write, by Kenneth Lewis Roberts
My Several Worlds: A Personal Record, by Pearl Buck
My Story, by Mary Roberts Rinehart
Not So Wild a Dream, by Eric Sevareid

Sports

Babe Ruth Story, by Babe Ruth, as told to Bob Considine
Lou Gehrig, a Quiet Hero, by Frank Graham
My Life In Baseball: The True Record, by Ty Cobb, with
    Al Stump
This Life I've Led, by Babe Didrikson Zaharias
Veeck—as in Wreck, by Bill Veeck with Ed Linn

Nursing

Angel of the Battlefield: The Life of Clara Barton, by Ishbel Ross

And They Shall Walk: The Life Story of Sister Elizabeth Kenny in collaboration with Martha Ostenso

Florence Nightingale, by Cecil Blanche Woodham Smith

TV and Entertainment

The Funny Men, by Steve Allen

Nature

Road of a Naturalist: Wood Engravings by Paul Landacre, by Donald Culross Peattie

Military Service

John J. Pershing, General of the Armies, by Frederick Palmer

Architecture

Frank Lloyd Wright: an Autobiography, by Frank Lloyd Wright

Photography

Portrait of Myself, by Margaret Bourke-White

Invention

Edison: A Biography, by Matthew Josephson

Advertising

Taken at the Flood: The Story of Albert D. Lasker, by John Gunther

Social Work

Jane Addams of Hull House, by Margaret Tims

11

When It's College Ahead

IF you're hoping to go to college, start preparing now, because there will be competition nearly everywhere you turn. According to one poll, seven out of ten high school students today are planning on four years of college.

The survey, taken by the Institute of Student Opinion and sponsored by Scholastic Magazines, covered a sampling of 5,297 public, private, and parochial school students from seventh through twelfth grades in more than one hundred secondary schools in all sections of the country.

In the fall of 1964, over five thousand fully qualified applicants were turned down by the University of Illinois because of overflowing enrollments, and another four thousand applicants were turned away because they were considered unfit.

On the other side of the coin, occasional viewpoints soften the stress, however. One that's more reassuring (at the same time pointing up the competition) comes from Fred M. Hechinger, former education director of the *New York Herald Tribune*. In a Public Affairs Committee pamphlet called "Worrying About College?" Mr. Hechinger advises:

"The fear of being turned down by the dean of admissions at the college 'of my choice' (or by any college) is rapidly assuming the proportions of a national neurosis. A combination of parental and social pressures bolstered by an almost limitless volume of folklore, myths, and misconceptions threatens to turn the very thought of planning for college into a nightmare. This may not only cause unnecessary heartache; it also opens the door to the worst kind of wrong planning.

"Actually, the picture is not nearly so grim as it is often painted. Nor is there much mystery about the procedure of admission or about the reasons for rejection. A sound knowledge of the facts and a little common sense will do the trick in most cases."

To this we must add, "If you start planning early!"

Figures show that the average lifetime income of a person with four years of college is nearly twice that of someone with only four years of high school. A broad, general education helps you keep your eyes and your mind open to the opportunities around you. It also helps you read more rapidly, grasp salient points immediately and think things through thoroughly. As long as you keep it an ongoing process, it helps you to move ahead to the new specialities you need. The broad horizons in our world today make your best insurance for the future all the knowledge you can possibly absorb.

Most important of all, college makes possible a self-discovery you seldom get elsewhere, regardless of "See Yourself" sessions, your interest tests in school, and your other outlets for finding yourself. From your first semester until your final semester of college you expose yourself to a wide range of new and different circumstances, and windows open in your mind.

Despite everything in favor of it, college is not for everyone, so it's no disgrace if it's not for you! There will be other alternatives in the chapter that follows. However, if college is on your mind, check your qualifications now by taking the following "See Yourself" quiz. Write in your notebook or across a piece of paper "Yes" and "No" and put a check for each question in the proper column as you rate yourself.

"SEE YOURSELF" SELF-EXAMINATION TEST FOR COLLEGE QUALIFICATIONS

1. Have you made a scholastic record that shows a B—or better—average and puts you in the top section of your class? (This incidentally, is an excellent qualification, since many C and almost all D students fail to finish college even if they're admitted.)
2. In case you have to ask your teachers or principal to write you a letter of recommendation for your attitude and achievement, would the things they could say about you be something you could count on for a qualification?
3. If you're a Junior or Senior and have already taken your College Entrance Examination Board tests or other college admission tests, do your scores on such tests as the "Preliminary Scholastic Aptitude Test" or the "Scholastic Aptitude Test" show that you stand a good chance of doing successful work in college?
4. When you compare your past and present school experiences and accomplishments with the experiences and accomplishments of other students who've gone through school with you, do you feel you measure up in learning ability and potential?
5. Do you participate in extracurricular activities in both your school and community?
6. Are your study habits good and do you feel you have a reasonable amount of self-discipline?
7. Have you made sure that the courses and subjects you're taking in high school meet college entrance requirements?

8. Are you considered a good school citizen by teachers and other students?
9. Have you an intelligent answer to "Why do you want to attend college?"
10. Are you thinking of college as a place in which you'll learn and grow rather than a place in which you'll put in time to please your parents, maintain a status, put off working or catch a spouse?

When you're finished, count up your Yes's. Then tally up your score. And if you're hoping for college let's hope the score is high since you'll need lots of Yes's in order to get to college.

Standards come high when it comes to getting to college, but sometimes a late starter or an undiscovered good student is fortunate enough to click with a college that's willing to give potential students who never achieved in high school a chance to make good in higher education.

Aided by a Ford Foundation grant, Williams College, in Williamstown, Massachusetts, admitted into its Freshman class in 1963 a ten percent quota of students who were below the academic standards generally demanded by the school. The experiment, scheduled to run for ten years, was set up for the specific purpose of finding out whether marks alone, as measured through college boards, high school grades or other academic norms, should be the factor for college selection.

Naturally the underachieving students accepted for this program had to show promise of future growth, an extra something indicating that college would benefit them, and definite strength of character. As a result of their chance to try college, every one of them completed their first year. Several of them made the dean's list.

If you can't quite make lots of Yes's in the "See Yourself" quiz, yet hope to be college-bound, get to work immediately and decide to adopt college-level study habits at once!

Work hard at improving your English, mathematics, science, foreign languages and history. At the same time get involved in some of the cultural, athletic, student, and social organizations that a college admissions officer will want to see on your record.

Types of Colleges

1. *Liberal Arts Colleges*

Liberal arts colleges offer a four-year program that leads to a Bachelor of Arts or a Bachelor of Science degree. In these programs you major in one subject—English, art, or chemistry, for example. Liberal arts colleges offer pre-professional training for further work in graduate schools, should you decide on a career in such professions as medicine or law.

2. *Teachers' Colleges*

Teachers' colleges offer a four-year program designed to prepare students for elementary or secondary school teaching. The program usually leads to a Bachelor of Arts degree and, in some states, a Bachelor of Science degree. A teachers' college may be a separate institution or it may be the college of education of a large university.

3. *Universities*

Universities have several divisions. Among the divisions may be a college of liberal arts, a college of medicine, a school of education, a college of dentistry, an engineering school, and a college of business administration. The first four years of work at a university, leading to a bachelor's degree, are called "undergraduate study." Universities also offer advanced, or graduate, study leading to masters' and doctors' degrees.

4. *Junior Colleges*

Junior colleges offer a two-year course of study at the college level. They provide either a preparatory or terminal course. But since we're concentrating on four-year colleges in this chapter, we'll postpone discussing junior colleges until the next chapter, because they can be an alternative when a four-year college career isn't planned. The same thing is true of two-year community colleges.

5. *Evening Colleges*

In evening colleges students work during the day and attend classes at night. This kind of college takes twice as long, of course, and the student has a big load to carry, but it offers the advantage of spreading college costs over a long period of time and combining practical work experience with study.

6. *Co-op Colleges*

Colleges offering cooperative education also combine practical work experience with study. More than fifty colleges offer this type of education, and a degree follows a four- to six-year program. Northeastern University, Fairleigh Dickinson, Antioch College, and the University of Denver are a few examples of the colleges offering this kind of study.

The study-training program offers alternate periods of attending college with periods of working in government, business, or industry. During employment periods students are paid standard wages.

For more detailed information on this kind of program, write to the National Commission for Cooperative Education, 8 W. 40th Street, New York, New York. 10018.

Your school guidance office will have many college catalogues on hand that you can start studying now. In addition, college directories such as *Lovejoy's College Guide* list and describe colleges and universities according to state. After checking these directories you can write for catalogues to the colleges that appeal to you.

As you look at catalogues, check such things as entrance requirements, costs, courses, faculty members, number of students, and college rules.

Choose the Right College

In applying to colleges you may take your choice from 2,000 of them, but it is most important that you choose the schools that fit your interests, personality, preparation, and intellectual capacity. If you haven't a special interest yet, despite the soul-searching you've already done, consider a general course at a liberal arts college. That will give you basic preparation. If you need to, you can do your specializing later.

In choosing the right college you'll also need to consider, in addition to costs, such things as

■ Whether or not you'll feel more at home on a large or small campus.

■ Whether you can achieve and keep up with the school's standards once you pass the entrance gates, or whether you'd be better in a school where the pressure is not so great. For example, if you study hard in high school and still can't get A's, you won't be happy in a hard-to-get-into college even if by some remote chance you gain admittance.

■ Whether you know in your heart that a coeducational campus will distract you too much from your work, or whether the normal atmosphere of boys and girls together will be a congenial atmosphere for working.

You'll hear a lot about "accredited colleges" while you're considering schools.

Actually, a stamp of accreditation simply means that a school meets the standards and qualifications of one of the six regional accrediting associations. When the school you choose is accredited, you can be sure that you can transfer your own credits from it to another institution and have them accepted. On the whole, a large majority of the colleges in the country are accredited. Their catalogues will specify the agency by which they're accredited.

Most of the time you'll be well advised to choose an accredited school. Some nonaccredited schools are not of a high enough quality to meet the accrediting association's standards. However, some others are nonaccredited simply because they're too new, too specialized, have too few volumes in their library, or for some similar reason. Often these colleges are less expensive and will take a student from the lower half of a high school class, although they may also have top-ranking high school graduates.

Before you decide on a nonaccredited school, get information about it by writing to the Council for the Advancement of Small Colleges, 1327 Eighteenth Street, N.W., Washington, D.C. 20036. Also, discuss the college with people in a position to advise you.

Whenever the subject of college comes up, someone always asks, "How will I know the right courses to take?" There's no single course in college that's the only "right" course for the future. But many men and women who have reached the top in their fields recommend a liberal arts course as a good beginning for many things.

That is because a liberal arts course gives a student a firm foundation, opens his eyes to much that's around him and provides him with a broad general base of learning. The broad base will pay off in later years, too, even if in the beginning you have to add a skill such as typing and shorthand, or another specialty, to your liberal arts background as your admission ticket to the job market.

If during your liberal arts course you decide where you're going job-wise, you can start specializing in your junior year.

College Costs

The cost of college varies, depending upon many factors. Usually expenses are highest in New England and the Middle Atlantic states, second highest in the Midwest, third highest in the West and lowest in the South. State universities and other publicly owned colleges usually cost considerably less than private institutions, though in most low-cost state universities the low tuition rates apply only to residents of the state.

Because costs vary and change rapidly, no table or chart of college costs is valid long enough to be listed in a book. The best way to find out the costs of the college of your choice is to write for specific fees.

Speaking generally, though, it costs some $10,000 to $12,000 to go through one of the country's top colleges today. You'll need half of this sum to foot the bill at a state university. At some colleges students spend well over $3000 a year. At others, it's possible to live on $1000 or less. The average student, however, spends over $2000.

As the competition for college entrance goes up, the costs go up, too. In fact, the Kiplinger Washington editors estimate that by 1970 costs for four years of college will range from $14,000 to $18,000 or more!

Paying for College

Unless your parents are so loaded with dollars and cents that money trees grow in your yard, they're going to need your help in putting you through college, so the sooner you figure out how to help, the better.

Students can pay for college—or help pay for college—through a combination of savings, scholarships, loans, and part-time employment. Here's a brief run of six ways to do it.

1. SAVINGS

Start saving now, if you haven't started already, by stashing away some of the dollars from your gifts and part-time jobs. In addition to saving your money, this also saves your face in college admissions offices, because admissions offices are often impressed by the young person who has worked and saved for college.

2. SCHOLARSHIPS

The basic requirements for a scholarship are high scholastic aptitude, superior high school grades, and strong potential for the future. The amount of a scholarship is usually determined by your financial needs. Other factors involved are your family's ability to pay, your mother's and father's salaries, your own earnings and assets, how many hours you can work while attending college, and how much money you can borrow. Scholarships are always a source of funds, of course. But generally, they're neither so plentiful nor so substantial that they can be counted on to any great extent. Presently, they're available in nearly a third of the states, and many business firms, churches, veterans' groups, and other organizations, including labor unions and professional associations, provide scholarship money.

State college scholarships are also a source of aid. You can find out about them by writing to your state department of education. The best way to find out about other scholarships is to write to the colleges of your choice and ask for a list of scholarships, plus information on how to apply for them. For more information on scholarships, consult the "Sources For Further Information" listed at the back of this book.

Once you have reviewed scholarship possibilities, apply for them early. The best time to obtain application blanks is in the fall of the year before you expect to start college. Then get references, transcripts and all other material you need and fill in and return the applications long before the deadlines.

3. *PACKAGED FINANCIAL AID FROM COLLEGES*

Today more schools than ever are giving financial aid to students who really need it. You can get details on this by writing to the College Entrance Examination Board, 475 Riverside Drive, New York, N.Y. 10027, and asking for the free booklet "Financial Aid for College—A Letter to Parents." (You can read it, too!) Also, as you write to individual colleges for catalogues, ask for their financial aid bulletin.

4. *LOANS*

Currently, loans are available to both students and their parents. Here are some to investigate.

The National Defense Student Loan Program

Under this program you can receive a loan on the basis of need in an amount up to $1000 a year, or a total of $5000. Repayment must begin one year after leaving school, with a maximum of ten years allowed for completing the payments. To receive a loan you must demonstrate both financial need and a good college aptitude. Special consideration is given to students who are preparing for a career in science, mathematics, engineering, modern foreign language, or teaching. For a list of colleges participating in the program, write to the United States Office of Education, Washington, D.C. 20202.

The United Student Aid Funds Program

One nonprofit organization, called United Student Aid Funds, Inc., offers a loan program providing sums under $1000 annually for three years. Local banks make the loans, and payments do not begin until several months after graduation. To find out more about this program and get a list of participating schools and banks, write to the United Student Aid Funds, College Square, Indianapolis, Indiana. 46206.

Other Types of Loans

Many states offer student loan plans, primarily for potential teachers and nurses. The state advances the money for training and the students "work it off" by pursuing their profession in the state. Your state department of education is your contact here.

Other possibilities—with your parents' assistance—are loans from a bank, credit union, insurance company, fraternal or other organization.

5. *SUMMER JOBS*

Over three million young people attending college earn a portion of their expenses, and one of the best ways of doing this is by working summers. The chapter in this book on summer jobs, plus other sources listed in the back of the book, will give you information on where to look for these jobs while attending high school and college. With good planning you may be able to make as much as $300 to $600 a summer during your college years.

6. *PART-TIME JOBS WHILE ATTENDING COLLEGE*

Many of the world's most successful people have worked their way through college—though today lots of educational authorities feel that those days are days of the past.

On the whole, these authorities are quick to advise that if you can possibly manage to avoid to burdening yourself with work as well as study for at least the first two years of college, your adjustment to college will be better.

If working is absolutely necessary, however, look into

the following jobs: tutor, stenographer, factory worker, laboratory assistant, gas station attendant, office worker, building and grounds helper, waiter, waitress, dishwasher, baby sitter, receptionist, sales clerk, research worker, usher, athletic department assistant, editorial assistant, dorm office helper, messenger, library worker, boarding hall worker, college store worker, janitor, student typist, faculty assistant, switchboard operator, or parking lot attendant.

With jobs such as these you may earn $500 during a year at college. When you're dependent upon these jobs, however, it's wise to write to the placement bureau of the college you plan to attend ahead of time and inquire what jobs will be available.

Tests for College Admission

Early in your Junior year, learn all you need to know about the necessity for taking tests for college admission. To get accurate information on the various scholarship qualifying tests and College Board tests you should take, consult your school or write to the College Entrance Examination Board, c/o Educational Testing Service, Box 592, Princeton, New Jersey 08540, and ask for the "Bulletin of Information" for the current year. You should also check college catalogues to determine what tests are required by the colleges you're considering.

Campus Visits and Interviews

Eleventh grade is a good time to visit campuses and have interviews. Here are some good guidelines for such visits from the University of Rochester:

Before deciding on your college-tour itinerary, ask one of your school's guidance counselors for his suggestions. His recommendations will help to guide you to the kinds of colleges that best meet your needs and interests.

Remember that summer isn't an "off-season" at the admissions office. If you want to talk with an admissions counselor, it's wise to make an advance appointment, if possible.

Dress comfortably. This means casual, spectator-type dresses for girls; perhaps informal sports shirts and slacks for boys. Admissions officers are human; they recognize that it's hard to look spic and span after a long, hot auto trip with the family small fry in tow. But you'll find it pays to stop off at a service station somewhere and freshen up a bit before arriving on campus. Don't hesitate to bring your parents. It's important for them to get a realistic impression of each college, too. Don't be afraid to ask an admissions counselor whether he thinks your qualifications are such as to make it worth while to file a formal application. It's important, of course, that you provide him with reasonably accurate information on your high school performance to date and your College Board scores.

If you're a high school Freshman or Sophomore you may find it helpful to tour campuses and pick up general admissions information that summer. However, it's better to wait until later in your high school career to schedule a formal admissions interview. Rochester's admissions officers find that a high school Sophomore can offer little of the objective data—such as College Board scores, comprehensive high school records, and so forth—that provide the "meat" of a formal admissions interview.

Remember that on many campuses the summertime student body is different in composition from the regular student roster. For example, the University of

Rochester runs a number of workshops, institutes and special summer programs that are attended by teachers and other professional people, as well as by undergraduate and graduate students from other colleges.

Don't try to cover too many colleges during a single trip. You'll be too rushed to get more than a fuzzy idea of each campus—and you and your family certainly won't have much of a vacation!

If you have time, take in some of the special events on campus. With many colleges operating full-steam-ahead throughout most of the summer, you're likely to find summer theatres, library and art exhibits, concerts, special lectures, and sports events listed on the campus calendar. You and your family will enjoy them—and they'll help to give you a more complete picture of college life.

After each visit make some notes on your reactions to the college. These can be extremely useful when you talk over your college plans with your school guidance counselor next fall.

Follow up your trip by talking with students in your area who attend the colleges you've visited. Summer is a good time to find some of them at home and to get their firsthand reactions to campus life. Alumni in your area will be glad to answer your questions, too.

If your tour raises some additional questions, don't hesitate to write for further information. But it's wise to check first to see whether such information may be provided in the catalogues and other literature which you received at each admissions office during your visit.

College Applications

By the time you're in twelfth grade it's a good idea to submit three or four applications if you're trying for the most selective colleges. On the other hand, if you're in the top half of your class and are applying for a state university, a local college that's not crowded, or a small college that's not well known, one or two applications should be enough.

If your heart is set on college, and you're in the bottom half of your class, be realistic enough to forget about the Ivy League and Top-Ten colleges. Instead make your applications to a selection of colleges likely to accept you and in which you'll be able to do the work. When you do this—with an average background in English, mathematics, history, and languages—there's always the possibility that some admissions officer will see the potential you may have and open the door to a college to you.

Getting Accepted vs Getting Turned Down

As you already know, getting accepted will depend to a large degree on

- How high your grades are
- How you rank in class
- How you score on college tests
- How well you're recommended by your school
- How well you project your personality in your interview

Besides these things, much will depend upon

- How well you fall into the desired geographical distribution of students desired by the school
- How full the courses for which you're applying happen to be

The last two factors are beyond your control and there's little you can do about them.

As for being turned down, there are two things you can do.

The first might be to follow the example of one young boy reported by the Johnson O'Connor Research Foundation and Human Engineering Laboratory.

The boy was told that with his high school record he couldn't possibly have any hope for getting into college, but he didn't take No for an answer.

Instead, he climbed into his old car and—on his own—visited a dozen colleges in the New Mexico, Arizona, and Texas area. As a result of his trip, he was accepted by one.

The second thing you can do if you get turned down by all the colleges to which you apply is to register with one of the nonprofit college admissions centers listed below. These centers are in touch with colleges that have vacancies; and when students apply to them, admissions personnel from accredited colleges with vacancies review the applications on file with the center and invite applications. Before applying to colleges with vacancies, though, you should follow through on all the procedures mentioned in this chapter.

College Admissions Centers

The College Admissions Assistance Center, 41 East 65th Street, New York, New York 10021. When you submit your application and transcript to this center your record is placed on file. Then colleges visit the center, see the official records on file, and get in touch with the students they believe will fit their criteria. The application fee is $15.00.

The Catholic College Admission Information Center,

3805 McKinley Street, N.W., Washington, D.C. 20015. This center matches a student's application form and records with the requirements of the colleges on file, and then everything about the student's record is sent to the colleges that might be interested in him. The student receives an application form directly from the college if a college is interested in him. The application fee is $15.00. *The College Admission Center,* 610 Church Street, Evanston, Illinois 60201. This center will help high school students who have not been accepted by a college in the spring of their graduating year. Admissions personnel from accredited colleges with vacancies review these applications on file with the center and invite applications from a high percentage. The application fee is $15.00.

How Well Will You Succeed in College?

In some cases staying in college is as big a challenge as getting into college, according to educational authorities. Nearly fifty percent of the freshmen who enter college so hopefully aren't around to graduate when degrees are awarded four years later! (Some of this large percentage, though, do get their degrees in some other way at some other time.)

What are the qualities and attitudes that you can take to college to insure your chances of staying there?

Here are five of the most important:

1. Go to get an education, not just a degree. Never shortchange yourself on the broad learning experiences you can get while there.

2. Be prepared to do more than the minimum when it comes to studying. The more you put into study the more your interest will grow—and the more your future will grow, too.

3. Know how to study before entering college.

4. Show a genuine interest in the life that goes on around you. Contribute something of yourself to it.

5. Take along with you the religious and moral values that were anchors in your home. College will challenge many of them. Expect that. It always happens. But in the long run the values that are challenged most are the ones that never really change in a changing world. They're anchors that are strong and good and footings for a firm future.

Hang on to them as you go!

P.S. to Girls

If it's wedding bells versus college bells, remember that by all standards, the easiest time in your life to crack the college books is when your parents help foot the bill and when you have only yourself to consider. It's true that women can go to college—and more and more of them may do it—when they have a family and home, but it's a whole lot easier when school is your whole job, and when you don't have to juggle schoolwork with home chores and babies, too.

P.S. to Boys

All males between eighteen and twenty-six are subject to the draft for military service under the Selective Service Act.

But if you make good grades in your first year of college and have a score of 70 or more on the Selective Service College Qualification Test, you'll probably be deferred until graduation. Your local draft board or the college you'll attend can give you full information on what to do and where you stand regarding your period of service.

12

When It's Not College Ahead

OF COURSE, four years of college is the right approach for everyone who's geared for college, but it isn't right for everyone who has a high school diploma. The right ticket is the kind of experience that will bring out the best in each person. College does this for some people. Other experience does it for others.

It's no disgrace not to go to college, either, any more than it's a disgrace to have blue instead of brown eyes. Figures tell us that at publication time nine million Americans of college age are not attending college.

When you lay your foundation for the future with hard work, good job skills and the right preparation for the right job for you there are many opportunities ahead that don't involve going to college. Take the case of a boy named Joe.

Joe was the son of a suburban family who had college degrees, a family business, wealth, and a home in the most expensive section in town. Because of this background everyone thought that Joe would go to college. But when he was ready to finish high school Joe suddenly made the shattering announcement that he intended to get an immediate job in the trucking business instead of entering college and preparing for a career in the family business.

The family argued and reasoned with him. His mother was completely crushed.

But Joe himself was determined! So, while the family ladled out advice, Joe maintained his confidence in his own decision about his future and got a job driving a truck for a suburban trucking firm. That crushed his family even more, and they said that he had no future.

But all the while they talked Joe grew more enthusiastic instead of less enthusiastic about his future.

From the first, he spent all his time away from his working shift driving overtime or hanging around the trucking firm's garage so he could learn more about trucking. As a result of his dedication to one thing, he saved enough money in a year to finance a small truck of his own and begin his own modest trucking business. Each year he bought additional trucks. And by the time he was thirty—through seeking the kind of experience that brought out the best in him—he had an expanding business of his own and a fleet of trucks, and lived with his lovely wife in his own beautiful home in the finest section of town.

Not everyone always does so well by the age of thirty, of course. But there are many ways to do well that don't require college, so examine the job possibilities in this chapter and find one for yourself. Some will open up to you as soon as you finish high school; others will need more training beyond your high school diploma. But there's a wide assortment here, and these are only a few of the possibilities before you.

Jobs Not Requiring Four Years of College

actor or actress	bank teller
aeronautical technician	barber
airline hostess	beautician and hairdresser
appliance serviceman	bookbinder
artist, commercial artist	book designer
assembler	bookkeeper
athlete	bricklayer
baker	broadcasting technician

bus driver or dispatcher
business machine serviceman
butcher
cabinetmaker
carpenter
cartoonist
cashier
caterer
civil service worker
clerk
clothing designer
construction worker
cook or chef
court reporter
credit manager
data processor
dental assistant
dental hygienist
designer
disc jockey
draftsman
dressmaker
drug wholesaler
electrician
electronic serviceman
engineering technician
entertainer or performer
farmer
file clerk
fishery technologist
floral designer
food distributor
food service personnel
food wholesaler or retailer
fund raiser
greeting card artist

guard or watchman
guide
heating and refrigeration
   technician
hospital attendant
hotel manager
illustrator
instrument worker
insurance agent
jeweler or watch repairman
laboratory technician
laboratory worker
library assistant
machinist
maintenance worker
manufacturer's sales representative
mason
mechanic
medical assistant
model
musician
nurse—practical or hospital-
   trained
nurses' aide
office machine operator
office supervisor
painter, plasterer, paper
   hanger
photographer
physical therapist
plumber
printer or photoengraver
private detective
programmer
proofreader

proprietor or owner of business

public stenographer

purchasing agent

radio announcer

real estate broker

receptionist

record jacket designer

recording technician

repairman

restaurant hostess

restaurant manager

salesman or saleswoman

secretary

service station attendant

service station manager

singer

sports announcer

stenographer

steward

store manager

tailor

tape recording technician

telephone operator

ticket agent

tool and die technologist

tool designer

traffic manager

travel agent

truck driver

typist

waiter or waitress

welder

window trimmer

writer

X-ray technician

Advance in These Jobs with Good Advanced Training

Despite the fact that the list you've just read points up many good jobs that don't require four years of college, the best jobs call for the right kind of training. For this reason, school shouldn't stop when you get your high school diploma. Education should be a lifetime project.

Most employers today favor the person with demonstrated learning ability who can be trained and retrained in a wide variety of skills. The available training is excellent, and some of it comes very close to college education. Here are twelve good opportunities.

Training Opportunities

1. *Two-Year Junior Colleges*

Nearly three-quarters of a million students attend junior colleges. Some of them were in the upper half of their high school class and purposely chose a junior college rather than a four-year college. Other students chose them because many junior colleges are easier to get into than a four-year college.

The programs in junior colleges are either preparatory or terminal. The preparatory course provides a broad liberal arts program for students who wish to go on to a four-year institution, or for those who want only two years of higher education. The terminal program offers specialized training for such semiprofessional fields as retailing, medical technology, secretarial work, and hotel management.

2. *Two-Year Community Colleges*

Most community colleges accept all high school graduates who want to continue their education. Usually they try to provide training in fields that will have job openings for their graduates, and the programs they offer are much like those described in the junior college programs listed above.

Students attending community colleges live at home, and the low tuition policy of the schools often makes it possible for students who couldn't attend college any other way to continue their education.

3. *Nursing Programs*

A hospital school of nursing will accept you directly from high school and prepare you for a Registered Nurse (R.N.) degree. Your course will last three years, and you'll get your training in classrooms, laboratories, and actual hospital work under medical supervision.

An alternative to studying nursing (in addition to the four- or five-year college progam in nursing) is the two-year nursing program offered in junior colleges. This requires two years of work, including summers. When the work is completed you're eligible to take the state examination for the Registered Nurse license.

If you are interested in becoming a practical nurse, you can take one of the twelve- or eighteen-month courses in practical nursing offered in hospitals, community agencies, or vocational schools.

4. *Vocational Training Schools*

In this country there are approximately four thousand schools that provide direct, practical training in a trade, craft, or skill. Their courses take anywhere from a few weeks to four years.

Typical of such schools are the ones that give training for business skills, hairdressing, barbering, printing, cooking, health service, and mechanical and technical jobs. There are both private and public vocational schools, and tuition fees vary widely.

The two directories for vocational training schools (Lovejoy's and Cohen's) listed in the back of this book will give you further information.

5. *Technical Institutes*

A technical institute offers a program of specialized training in preparation for such semiprofessional jobs as engineering aide, dental hygienist, X-ray technician, and electronic technician. Most programs provide two-year training periods.

There's a tremendous need for these jobs. The President's Committee on Scientists and Engineers says, "We are now graduating, through accredited and approved courses, less than one-sixth of the number of highly skilled scientific and engineering technicians that we need."

If there is a possibility here that appeals to you, you can send for a list of approved schools and programs from the National Council of Technical Schools, 1507 M Street, N.W., Washington, D.C. 20005.

6. *Evening Courses Combined With Full-Time Employment During the Day*

The courses you take at night while you work at a job by day can be anything you want to make them!

They may be the enrichment and fun courses—as well as the serious ones—found all over the country in YMCA's, YWCA's, community centers, adult education schools, evening schools, and university extension departments. On the other hand, they can be the kind of courses you take to improve your vocational opportunities.

In the past, many men and women who have moved up the ladder in jobs and careers have worked by day and gone to school by night. It's very possible that this can happen to you.

One person who found success and satisfaction this way was Gene Tway, youthful vice-president of Empire Crafts Corporation, one of the largest direct-selling corporations in the country.

At the end of his high school days Gene Tway found himself without any really clear-cut idea of what he wanted to do next. To tide him over until he found out, he took a job in an insurance agency in Wichita, Kansas, and enrolled in an evening school business course. Late at night and over weekends he let his hobby work for him by playing the clarinet or tenor sax in dance bands. While working at the latter job, he met his wife, Patti, a vocalist with one of the bands.

Patti's mother, the Kansas sales manager for a china and silver company, so constantly sang the praises of selling that Gene Tway decided to try it when he had a week's vacation from his other job.

The first week he sold china and silver he earned enough to make him feel that selling was the career for him. He put all his ambition and energy to work, gave up all other activities, and started to work full-time for Empire Crafts. A year later he became manager for the Wichita area. When his mother-in-law moved to Hawaii he became the Kansas sales manager. Then he moved into the company's home office as a regional sales manager, handling the southern part of the United States. A few years after that he was made general sales manager, and at the age of thirty-seven became vice-president of his company.

7. *The Armed Forces for Men*

Boys investigating military service under the Selective Service Act with their local Armed Forces representatives will find that there are many ways in which to handle the period of service. It can be both an educational and a vocational experience.

In case you're not aware of it, the Army is the only branch of service into which you can be drafted. You can enlist, however, in the Army, Navy, Air Force, Marine Corps, or Coast Guard. When you're drafted, you have no choice of assignment. When you enlist, you can select from the specific programs offered by each of the services.

Training is available in more than 250 career fields, including engineering, photography, transportation, communications, electronics, and guided missiles, to cite just a few examples. All of them provide excellent preparation for related civilian occupations, so you may improve your skills for later civilian life during your period of service. At the same time, your opportunities for off-duty, nonmilitary education are excellent. With your parents, teachers, clergyman, employer and armed forces representative, weigh the advantages of enlisting at a very early age against the advantages of waiting for the draft.

8. *The Armed Forces for Women*

There are approximately 35,000 women in all branches of the Armed Forces. All of them are enlisted, since women are not drafted. A large majority serve overseas.

To be eligible for the service, a girl needs a high school education or the equivalent, and she must be no less than eighteen. She must be unmarried, have no dependents, be in good health and have high moral standards. If she is under twenty-one she needs her parents' or guardian's written permission. Enlistment periods vary, according to the branch of service.

Happily, training in specific career fields is open to women, too. But before you enlist you should make every effort to find out whether the service of your choice offers the career fields that interest you.

Full information on vocational and educational opportunities can be obtained by visiting your local recruiting office or by writing to the Defense Advisory Committee on Women in the Service, OASD (MP&R) the Pentagon, Washington, D.C. 20301.

9. *Home Study or Correspondence Courses*

Both private correspondence schools and colleges give general education and vocational courses by correspondence. When you enroll in these courses you work on assignments designated by the school. When the assignment is completed, you mail it back to the school. There it's checked and corrected by one of the instructors. When you put a great deal into home study courses you often get a great deal out of them.

One young high school graduate whose story was reported in *Seventeen* was interested in fashion illustration and got a job after high school with a pattern company. But her heart was set on real fashion drawing and she saw no immediate chance for that in the job she had. So while still holding her job, she enrolled in a correspondence course in commercial art with the Famous Artists Schools.

A few months later she was able to take advantage of a new opportunity that opened for her as an illustrator for a New York resident buying office. Later, she became assistant art director.

If home study or correspondence courses interest you,

you can be sure you are selecting an accredited school by writing to the National Home Study Council, 1601 Eighteenth Street, N.W., Washington, D.C. 20009, for their free "Directory of Accredited Schools and Courses."

The Cohen and Lovejoy directories also include lists of schools offering home study. Another publication, "Guide to Correspondence Study," published by the National University Extension Association, is in your library and will give you more help.

10. *On-the-Job Training*

On-the-job training is provided by many businesses and industries, including retailing, banking, insurance, sales, and clerical work.

When you take full advantage of trainee and company programs this type of education offers you opportunities to learn new skills or improve old ones. Training courses cover a variety of subjects that relate to a company's products and services. Offices of your State Employment service, as well as private employment agencies, can give you specific information about on-the-job training opportunities in your area.

11. *Apprenticeship Training Programs*

An apprentice enters into an agreement with an employer to learn a particular trade.

Actually, apprenticeship is one of the oldest forms of on-the-job training in existence, and today apprentice programs are offered by more than ninety different trades, but most apprenticeship training programs are found in the building, printing, mechanical repair, and machine trades.

When a person is accepted for apprenticeship, a contract stating the terms and conditions of his training is registered with the state apprenticeship council. His working conditions and training courses are specified and he is taught by experienced craftsmen.

His earnings begin at no less than half the full-scale wages in the trade. And when he is accepted into the craft union at the end of his training period he is paid full union scale. Information on this type of job training can be obtained from the Department of Labor, Bureau of Apprenticeship and Training, Washington, D.C. 20210.

12. *Self-Education*

This training opportunity takes a lot of self-discipline, but from the beginning of time there have been successful people who taught themselves.

A ticket to the future through self-education involves a lot of planned reading, plus stimulating associations with live groups that share your interests. Often such groups are to be found in community and church organizations. Traveling is a third route to self-education. A fourth is attending lectures and discussions and visiting art galleries and museums.

Pick the Right School or the Right Course

Many of the things we discussed when we talked about selecting colleges also pertain to selecting the right training opportunities when you are not planning to go to college. But here are six extra pointers:

1. Be sure you have sufficient skill, aptitude and interest in the subject you're considering to make the course meaningful to you. Even the best practical training in the world won't fulfill your hopes for it until you have something to bring to it yourself.

2. Check all courses and all schools before you investigate one thoroughly. Sources to check are the approved lists published by state departments of education, directories such as Lovejoy's and Cohen's references mentioned in this chapter, and trade and professional associations in the field that especially interests you. Your library can give you names and addresses of these associations.

3. If you're taking a course for credits, make sure that you are enrolled in an accredited school.

4. Before you enroll, ask the school for names and addresses of a cross-section of graduates now working at jobs. If the school is proud of its record you'll get the names. Ask the graduates how they made out in their courses, how they got their jobs, and what standing the school had when they looked for a job.

5. As you solicit information, pay attention to the type of places where graduates are working. List the names and addresses of similar places of employment where you might work in your area. Later, get in touch with the people who do the hiring there and ask if the course you're considering is accredited for a job with them.

6. Find out about the fee-paying policy of the school before you enroll. Has it a full-payment-in-advance-with-no-refunds policy? Or is it based on a weekly or monthly pay-as-you-go tuition basis?

Jobs for High School Graduates

If you're ready to enter the job world after graduating from high school, go back to Chapters I and II and "See Yourself" now as you saw yourself then. By doing this you can keep in mind the role you want as you seek your first job. Refresh your mind on the pointers in Chapters IV, V, and VI.

Temporary Jobs

If—despite the "See Yourself" tests and other helps you've had—you're still unsure of yourself and what you want from your future, you might consider taking a series of temporary jobs to help you find yourself and discover what career you want to follow.

Generally speaking, no temporary job service is especially interested in encouraging teenagers to apply. What they want most is seasoned, experienced people. But occasionally boys and girls just out of school do get jobs through temporary personnel services if they have certain skills.

If they come from a commercial school they can start with secretarial jobs. Those with such rudimentary office skills as typing can use them. Those with no experience whatsoever can start as clerks. There is a good demand for clerks.

A temporary personnel service of this sort gives you a painless introduction into the business world. Through temporary jobs you can shift from job to job in different industries and businesses and find out whether one field or another is better suited for you.

One young high school graduate for whom this kind of introduction to the job world worked well had a physical defect and so little confidence in herself that she felt there was little way for her to plan on a job and future. But she had excellent typing skills, so she forced herself to apply at an agency.

She did very well with several temporary jobs. Then, with the money she earned, she bought the first attractive clothes she had ever owned. This compensated for her physical handicap immeasurably and made her feel so much better about herself that after a while she began to save everything she could from her earnings so she could pay for a course in a fashion institute and plan for a future working in that field.

Her interests in her future replaced her diffidence with confidence as she found that (1) she did a good job on every temporary job and that (2) people liked her wherever she was sent to work. The temporary jobs made it possible for her to work some days and go to school the other days.

Such a happy story can be yours, too, if you make up

your mind to grow and develop to the best of your abilities through all the experience and training you can give yourself, and if you plan with all your heart to fulfill your own best image of yourself. From the moment you begin to become what it's in you to be, nobody cares whether you went to college or not!

13

Summer Jobs

"How on earth can you get an 'in' for a worthwhile summer job?" is a question teenagers ask frequently.

Actually, there are no "in's." Instead, you just get busy and hunt for your own summer work.

There are excellent reasons why working in the summer pays off.

1. A summer job provides you with money for clothes, education, and other necessities.

2. It teaches you how to get along with different types of people from those you associate with at home or at school. At the same time it gives you an opportunity to meet new friends and exchange ideas, experiences, ideals, and knowledge.

3. It makes you feel good "inside" because you're able to earn some money on your own.

4. It gives you valuable work experience.

5. It gives you a chance to travel and see a different part of the country, if you're old enough to get a job that takes you away from home.

6. It provides you with a chance to have fun, since a summer job gives you vacation opportunities at the same time it gives you work.

7. It provides you with a commitment and a system of discipline.

8. It gives you something to show for your two months of summer vacation.

9. It offers you the chance to try several job fields through different kinds of jobs.

10. It lets you sample the job field where you hope to have a career.

One person who took a summer job and ended up with a full-sized career in the job field of his choice was a boy named Gary Press. While still a student, Gary, who wanted to get into television, landed a job with Goodson and Todman for the summer. Here is his story:

"My first summer job in television involved running errands, typing scripts, opening mail, and doing miscellaneous chores. The next summer I did the same kind of jobs.

"But after I graduated from college, I had my foot in the door at Goodson and Todman, so I went to work for them on a full-time basis on their program 'Password.' In that job I did such things as hold cue cards for Allen Ludden, the M.C. of the program, and help in the coordination of the art work used on the air. After eight months on 'Password' I became casting director of the night-time version of 'To Tell The Truth.' Then, after two years on 'To Tell The Truth,' I joined a new show, 'Get The Message,' as program coordinator."

Another person who furthered his development in a career field through a summer job was John Fox of Stuart, Florida.

From the time John was seven nature had been his hobby. At first it was merely a pastime, but in his second year in high school his teacher suggested that he make a study of green turtles. That was his first serious project.

As a result of this project John worked at a museum and marine aquarium the following summer. Ultimately he won a Westinghouse Science Talent Search Award and a prize of $250 for his study of stone crabs. Later, he enrolled at Johns Hopkins University with the career aim of becoming a researcher in marine biology.

Essentially, there are two kinds of summer jobs: working for an outside employer, and self-employment.

On the whole, the summer opportunity for outside employment is greater for high school Seniors and college students than for teens sixteen and younger because of the labor laws that prohibit boys and girls under eighteen from taking many types of jobs. But when you're of employable age you'll find your main opportunities are jobs with business and industrial firms, resort hotels, restaurants, Boy Scouts, Girl Scouts, YMCA's, YWCA's, the Federal government, national and state parks, swim clubs, hospitals, museums, motels, summer theaters, and amusement parks.

One man who made a summer job grow into a big main act is Irving Rosenthal, owner of the world-famous, multimillion-dollar Palisades Amusement Park, atop the New Jersey Cliffs.

As youngsters, Rosenthal and his brother Jack borrowed fifty dollars and went to work selling pails and shovels on the beach at Coney Island. By the end of the summer the boys had made a handsome $1500 profit. For many summers after that, Rosenthal continued to work at amusement parks not only to help his family but also to work his way through dental school.

After reaching that goal, he decided, after all, that he loved the zoom of the roller coaster better than the buzz of the dentist's drill, and eventually he worked right up to the ownership of a huge amusement park.

Summer Job Opportunities

Other places where business increases in the summer and where you might look for a job are:

bowling alleys
country clubs
miniature golf courses
fishing boats and piers
yacht clubs
travel bureaus
car hop stands
souvenir stands
ice cream stores
ice cream manufacturers
fishing tackle stores
sporting goods shops
camera and hobby shops
driving and rifle ranges
country fairs
sightseeing bus and boat
    lines
motion picture theaters
community centers
dude ranches
farms
settlement houses
landscaping services

greenhouses
recreation centers
carpet and rug cleaners
garages
zoological and botanical
    gardens
orchards
pet shops
libraries
soda bottling plants
candy factories
distribution services for
    catalogues and samples
baseball parks
car washes
airline terminal concessions
bus terminal concessions
railroad concessions
furniture repair shops
upholsterers
furnace, stove and
    chimney cleaners
painting contractors

maintenance department of
  colleges
parking lots
service stations
construction companies
engineering firms
home servicing companies
air conditioning companies
awning repair shops
surveying companies

dry cleaning stores
ice and ice cube companies
food stores
drugstores
toy factories
canneries
packing houses
messenger and telegraph
  services
vending machine companies

Typical Jobs Available

Typical jobs available at these places of employment are kitchen helper, porter, waiter, waitress, chambermaid, counter attendant, bus boy, bellboy, countergirl; bookkeeper, stenographer, telephone operator, typist, clerical worker, receptionist, messenger, telegraph operator; store clerk, supermarket checker, stock boy, cashier, salesgirl; service station attendant; drive-in attendant or carhop; guide or demonstrator; usher or usherette; ticket taker or ride attendant at amusement parks; maintenance worker at summer enterprises; baby sitter and mother's helper for families vacationing for the summer; tutor; library attendant; laboratory assistant; engineering aide; survey worker; farm worker, produce picker or produce packer; greenhouse worker; window washer; laborer, handyman, yard worker or janitor; playground assistant, swim club or pool worker, park or beach helper, swimming instructor or lifeguard; golf caddy; state park employee.

Special Mention: Camp Jobs

Most camp jobs—a special favorite in summer employment—require young people of eighteen or nineteen with some college background. But there are exceptions to every rule, and when you're a diligent job hunter you can sometimes find junior counselor jobs when you're sixteen or seventeen.

David Leith of Ohio, who got a camp job as a junior counselor for two summers, tells his story this way:

"The summers my friend David DeHaven and I were sixteen and seventeen we secured employment as junior counselor at camps in New Hampshire. The job opportunities we received were listed in the 'Summer Employment Directory.' To get the jobs we sent letters of application and personal data sheets to about twelve prospective employers. Both of us asked to be considered together for the positions we desired.

"Quite a few employers replied that we were too young. Others sent their own application forms to be filled out. Then came the anxious period of waiting.

"The first contact was made late in December. But it was March before a job offer actually came through. The first summer, we worked at Boston University Camp Sargent at Peterborough, and there was no salary. The next summer, we took jobs at Camp Woodbrook at Fitzwilliam, and we each earned $75.00.

"Working at a camp is an experience that demands elasticity of the individual. Sometimes it means rising at 7:00 A.M. in a 30° temperature to get a tentful of kids out of their warm bunks and start the day.

"At other times our duties were to clear fields and haul away the brush; build basketball areas by digging the post holes, setting the post to hold the backboard, and putting up the basket; repair cabins or the wooden tent floors; or do other maintenance work.

"But these things, coupled with the monetary benefits of salary plus room and board, made a job at camp a worthwhile way to spend the summer. In addition to learning how to get along with people, this job gave us a chance to see a different part of the country, be out of doors all summer and enjoy nature to the fullest extent."

To David Leith's words his friend David DeHaven adds, "When the campers left after the camp season was over I felt a bit of sadness. But the fact that I had helped someone have a very worthwhile and rewarding summer made my experience enriching and wonderful. I only hope that I can do it again for many summers to come."

Special Mention: Direct Selling

Door-to-door selling has spelled "jobs and futures" for many generations of young people. Although today some of the firms in the direct selling field tend to hire only older teenagers, some—Stanley Home Products, for example—report that they do offer opportunities to high school students. As a matter of fact, that firm has a record of one boy who began selling Stanley products when he was twelve years old, and worked with the company right through high school.

Another girl started selling products while in high school and each year did better than the year before. Ultimately, she did so well that she won savings bonds, scholarships and other prizes for her sales, and—while still in high school—became a group leader for as many as forty-two other students.

How Do You Hunt for a Summer Job?

Begin looking early, however, because there are more summer workers who need jobs than there are summer jobs that need workers. Automation, vacations every month of the year and temporary employment services all take their toll of summer jobs. Consequently, the winter and spring months are not a bit too soon to look for summer work.

While you're looking, keep your mind open to several choices, too, since you may have to take what's available.

Whatever you gain in experience, though, will always be useful to you.

In general, summer job hunts should follow the same procedures discussed in Chapters IV, V and VI, so refer to those sections often. Besides that, keep the following pointers in mind:

1. Ask your friends, relatives, neighbors, former employers or employers for whom your family has worked whether they know of any summer job prospects.

2. Read the "Help Wanted" ads in your newspaper regularly. Consult the classified directory of your telephone book for names and addresses of specific companies or firms in your community. Inquire about summer jobs at your school and the office of your local state employment service.

3. Write a good letter of application. According to experts in the employment field more summer jobs are obtained by a letter of application than by any other means.

Here's a guide to follow for yours—and be sure to include the dates you're available for employment.

SAMPLE SUMMER JOB APPLICATION LETTER

Street
City
Date

Mr. Robert Cook
Cook's Department Store
Smithtown, Missouri

Dear Mr. Cook:

I should like to apply for a summer job as a clerk in one of the departments of your store. I will be available for employment at any time from June 25 to September 1.

At the present time I am a Senior in _____ High

School. I'm planning to enter college in the fall to prepare for elementary school teaching.

Between my Junior and Senior years in high school I worked in a small dress shop, where I gained valuable experience in meeting people and selling clothes. Prior to that experience I sold Christmas cards and magazine subscriptions from door to door.

My other experience and qualifications, along with my photograph, personal data, and references, are listed fully on the attached résumé.

Thank you for considering me. I am enclosing a self-addressed stamped envelope for your reply. If it's more convenient, you can reach me for an interview by calling 111-2222.

Very truly yours,
Your name in ink

If neither you nor your parents are acquainted with some place where you're seeking summer employment and would like to know more about it, the local office of your State Employment Service will give you advice about the reputation of a little-known firm. Also, you can receive a report on the firm by checking with the Better Business Bureau or chamber of commerce in the city or town where the firm is located.

Self-Employment

If you're under sixteen, your best chance to work may be self-employment, and usually the best way to promote your project is to canvass your neighborhood, as well as small stores and businesses, to see what services you can perform.

The educational department of the Royal McBee Corporation reports that by using this method high school Sophomore Terry Coffey got a job addressing envelopes at

a penny each, for advertising purposes, for a local busi-
nessman; Merry Lou Fellows found a job typing verse for
her poet uncle; and Janet Katz typed rent receipts and
bills for a real estate office in her neighborhood for a few
hours daily.

Other job possibilities available to students who want
to earn money through typing, according to Royal McBee's
research, are typing themes and papers for college professors and students, typing and cataloguing cards in libraries, typing and mimeographing menus for restaurants,
typing for ministers and church organizations, and typing
for fraternal organizations and business clubs. To find
your share of such jobs, write each potential employer a
letter telling him of your availability. Type up cards announcing your service and distribute them widely. Also,
make personal calls whenever you can.

Paying personal calls—and keeping your eyes wide
open as you call—can sometimes pay off handsomely,
too.

While he was looking for summer work, twelve-year-old
Don White knew he'd like to do something with his talent
for art, but he also knew it wouldn't be easy for a twelve-
year-old boy to get a job as an artist. So Don kept his eyes
and ears open and made as many personal calls as he
could. While he was looking for work one day, the proprietor of a local luncheonette offered him a job washing
dishes.

"Why don't I draw new signs for you instead?" Don
suggested, indicating the signs above the counter. "Take
that 'Ham 'n Eggs' sign, for instance. I bet I could design
something that would really make your customers want to
buy some ham and eggs."

"You're in business for twenty-five cents a sign," the
proprietor told him.

Once Don realized he had a good, salable service, he

decided to do all he could about it. Between sign-painting sessions for the luncheonette he went on a door-to-door campaign to solicit orders from both businesses and homes. Some people gave him an order just because they were amused at the whole idea, but when they saw how serious Don was and how clever he was with the signs, they helped him find more business.

As a result, before many weeks were over, the twelve-year-old boy who had started his business for 25¢ a sign was getting $4 to $5 for some of his signs.

Possibly you're not either an artist or a typist—and certainly not everyone is! But there are other job services you can create in addition to the usual baby-sitting, ironing, or caring for gardens and lawns that young people do in the summer.

Other possibilities are a job as an apartment or house caretaker, car washer, cleaner of attics and basements, dish washer, golf caddy, mail box painter, pet walker and sitter, tree pruner, party planner, children's companion, and junk collector. (You can sell the junk you collect to dealers and collectors for good prices.)

Services you might consider are a general delivery service, a newspaper and magazine delivery service, a shoe-shine service, a floor waxing service, or a sewing and mending service.

When you set up a service, make it known by any or all of the following methods: word of mouth, newspaper advertising, notices on community boards, or mimeographed letters that you distribute from door to door or circulate among your friends.

Here is a letter one teenager devised and used that was published in *National Hi-Y Boys Magazine*. You may want to use it as a model for your own.

NAME

ADDRESS

PHONE NO.

DATE

Dear Neighbor:

That extra right arm you've been longing for is now available.
I am ready to take on all kinds of small or large, important or
unimportant jobs. Check those of the following that indicate
your needs and call me at the above number for immediate
service.

———————— Chauffeuring (any kind, younger members to clubs,
tennis lessons, summer school, playgrounds, movies,
dates, etc.).

———————— Marketing. I can do all that dreary shopping at your
favorite emporium and deliver right to the proper
place on your shelves.

———————— Cleaning and organizing materials in garages, basements, and attics.

———————— Pruning trees and shrubs.

———————— Painting. (I won't offer to paint the house or your
living room, but I can paint shutters, benches, out-
door furniture, etc.).

———————— Bicycles. I can teach young people to ride.

———————— Barbecue or Party Handy Man. I can serve food and
drinks, handle kids, clean up, etc.

———————— Baby-sitting, of course.

———————— Vacation Handy Man. While you're away I can
water lawns and indoor plants, check your home,
forward mail and do chores.

———————— Tennis lessons for young beginners.

———————— Tutoring in most subjects through junior high level.

———————— Kid care. Figure on me to read aloud, organize
games, and help them pass the hours with profit.

———————— Personal Messenger Service—to and from our town,
and elsewhere.

_____ Miscellaneous. You fill it in. I probably can do it. Rates reasonable—depending on job, duration, and work involved.

Age: _____

Usually the best way to figure out your rates is to work by the hour or by the job. Find out what other people in your community get for similar work. Also, get advice from your parents and business acquaintances. By all means, though, charge rates that are in line with your experience and ability. Overcharging will get you no jobs fast!

When you establish your rates let your clients know ahead of time what the charges will be.

Make the most of your summer work. One boy who did was a high school Junior who located a job one summer selling plants and garden supplies in the landscaping department of a supermarket. He needed college money— all that he could get—but he wasn't particularly enchanted with the supermarket job he found. In fact, he couldn't convince himself that the paths among the evergreens could ever be paved with opportunity! Nevertheless, he lived by the working philosophy that when you do your best on every day's work you never know what you'll find.

And it paid off, too. When he had been at the supermarket job only a short time a woman came in one day and bought $150 worth of evergreens. The boy spent a lot of time with her while she made her selections and then, while she was paying for the plants, he heard her mumble to herself, "Now, all I have to figure out is how to get them planted!"

Since he was keeping his eyes and ears open for other jobs he could do, he immediately offered to go to the woman's house and plant the evergreens in his spare hours. The happy ending came about because he went to the woman's house and did his best again—all without having any possible way of knowing that the woman's husband was vice-president of the supermarket chain that was employing him.

Both the woman and her husband were delighted with everything about him, and before he had finished planting the $150 worth of evergreens, they offered him a job at their home the rest of the summer at a much more remunerative salary than he was earning down at the store.

Now he had a job contract that could help him for the rest of his life!

14

Summer Activities That Pay Off in Experience

IF collecting dollars from summer jobs is not vital for you this year, there are other things to do to make your summer pay. Some of the most exciting—if you're lucky enough to have the opportunity—are studying, traveling, or working abroad.

The Institute of International Education, a clearing

house for information on study programs abroad, reports that today's teenagers are no longer waiting till they're of college age to take summer courses in art, music, history, and other subjects in cultural centers like Florence, Geneva, and Paris. Some combine studying and touring. Others work on farms, then tour high spots overseas both during and after the work period.

One high school girl spent six weeks working on a collective farm in Israel, with interesting side trips to Tel Aviv, Jerusalem, Mt. Carmel, Mt. Zion, and the Sea of Galilee. She went water skiing on the Red Sea. On her way home she visited Genoa, Rome, Florence, Geneva, and Paris.

Another high school girl spent the summer of her Junior year studying at the University Clermont-Ferrand in France with many other students from different countries and finished the season with visits to Switzerland and England.

There are special student tours abroad by boat or plane (and then by bus and train); youth hosteling trips through Europe by bicycle; and a program called the "Experiment in International Living" in which young people of sixteen or older spend several weeks in one community abroad, living with a family, speaking their language, and joining in group activities with other teenagers in town. Under the guidance of trained leaders, these young people live in a private home and share the everyday life of the family. In addition to this day-by-day living experience, they have an opportunity to take informal trips to other parts of the country.

Organizations that can provide further information are listed in the "Sources of Further Information" section at the end of this book.

Another travel opportunity is presented by the American Field Service exchange program, which provides eight weeks in the summer (or a full school year) living with a family in a foreign country.

Applicants for this program are asked to answer an endless number of questions on such topics as health, interests, and hobbies. They are also required to submit essays on such subjects as a typical day in summer, a description of family members, and a description of family relationships.

They need many personal qualifications, too. The American Field Service says that each high school student chosen for this opportunity must be intelligent, tactful, neat, attractive, cooperative, stable, poised, helpful, reliable, alert, and thoughtful—with a sense of humor thrown in as an extra. Such qualities are highly important because, for the period he is abroad, one of the student's jobs will be to represent his country well.

Students are sent to any one of thirty-nine foreign countries, including Afghanistan, Turkey, Malaysia, Pakistan, and Uganda. The choice is made by the selection office of the American Field Service in New York City. Often there are many more applications than the program can accomodate, and only the best-qualified students are considered, so early planning is vital.

If you are interested in exploring such opportunities, your first step should be a thorough check with your school and community to see what's available through them and what you must do to qualify.

Information on the American Field Service program can be obtained from its office at 313 East 43d Street, New York, New York 10017. Other places to write for information on other programs are listed in the back of this book.

Outside these sources, a wealth of information on working, studying, and traveling abroad (for the school year or summer vacation, and for high school and college students) is published in material that you can obtain by writing to the United States National Student Association, 265 Madison Avenue, New York. 10016. Two particularly informative books available from this organization are *Work, Study, Travel Abroad* and *Exciting Student Tours Abroad*. Each lists many opportunities and sells for a nominal fee.

Preparing for the Peace Corps

No list of opportunities for working, studying, or traveling abroad—and no discussion of jobs and futures—would ever be complete without a reference to the Peace Corps. It provides work for the kind of person who wants to give as well as get—whose concern for the future includes other peoples' futures, too!

As you probably know, a member of the Peace Corps is sent where he's needed to work in the villages, mountains, factories, or towns of struggling, newly developing areas. But as he gives, he also gains, by adding to his own experience.

The minimum age for Peace Corps Volunteers is eighteen, and the minimum education is a high school diploma, although most of the volunteers are college graduates or people who have had college training.

Naturally, you can't play a role in the Peace Corps for the brief span of a summer vacation. But if you're thinking of it for part of your future, as many young people are, you can spend a summer during your high school years preparing yourself for this service.

These suggestions to school students interested in joining the Peace Corps from Frank W. Erwin, deputy director of selection for the Peace Corps, originally appeared in the *American Red Cross Journal:*

1. Learn a second language. Ability in a foreign language is not required of applicants, but it is a great help. French and Spanish are particularly useful.

2. Take part in community activities. Experience as a camp counselor and participation in the youth volunteer service activities offered by many organizations are considered valuable.

3. Choose hobbies and recreation in which you learn to work with others. People are the key to Peace Corps projects. Anything that helps you reach people—an interest in sports, music, dramatics, or what-have-you—could help make you valuable to the Peace Corps. Versatility and adaptability are very important.

If you're interested in learning more about the Peace Corps and your chance to be a part of it, write to The Peace Corps, Washington, D.C. 20525.

Summer Study at Home

Since obtaining a useful education is the main job of young people, you can make your summers pay by attending summer school in order to

- Make up work you failed or couldn't take during the regular school year
- Take courses that you need for college entrance requirements
- Complete your high school program in less than the normally required time
- Take courses that will give you more background for getting jobs or add to your general knowledge and background
- Accumulate college preparatory credits

Before you select your courses for summer school you'll usually find it to your advantage to discuss your plans with your teachers. Because of their experience they may be able to suggest courses that will fit your specific needs.

In addition to the summer programs many high schools provide, private schools and colleges also operate summer school programs, and many camps throughout the country combine a study or cultural program with a camping program. Your local library will have directories for camps and schools that have summer courses, so seek your librarian's help in consulting them.

Skills That Will Earn Money

Typing is a learning you can turn to earning almost any time you want to!

Actually the experiences of people who have done this—often during the summer—could fill the rest of this book, but the success of two New England boys will suffice as an example.

They had been persuaded, against great resistance, to learn to type. Typing was far removed from any future career plans of theirs, "But learn typing anyhow," they were advised. "You'll hang on to more money in college when you can type your own notes."

Just what this meant they couldn't possibly know until they hit a university town and found that there was a tremendous shortage of typists compared with the number of students who needed papers typed.

The boys decided—strictly on impulse—to rent a tiny vacant store and set up a typing service. Then they spread the word that they were in business. By managing their off-hours cooperatively so they could conduct their business, they not only earned enough money to pay a substantial part of their expenses but also profited enough so that they could buy themselves the kind of cars most college boys dream about. School students do benefit by acquiring some commercial skill.

Correspondence Courses

Summer correspondence courses can pay dollar dividends. A course in any of the following fields can develop your moneymaking skill: art, automotive, diesel, commercial, drafting, electrical, radio, electronics, graphic arts, machine trades, radio and TV programing, salesmanship, or advertising.

In a supervised correspondence course you can work at your own speed. But finishing a course can be your summer project and you may find one that helps lead to a future career.

If you'd like information on the right correspondence course for you, you can write to the National Home Study Council, 1601 18th Street, N.W., Washington, D.C. 20009.

15

Volunteer Jobs

STILL another way to make a productive and worthwhile two months of your summer is to look into the possibility of doing volunteer work for some community agency. The working experience may influence you in the choice of your career, and the inner satisfaction you'll get from such work will pay you, in its own way, as well as dollars and cents.

Some typical summer jobs that teenage volunteers take over are jobs working with physically and emotionally handicapped children; assisting in hospitals, baby clinics, and nursing homes; shopping for shut-ins; acting as club leaders for boys' and girls' clubs; helping at settlement houses and with church youth groups; participating in conservation projects; and preparing wall maps to show areas in the United States served by a Red Cross blood program.

Look for such opportunities for service in your town by going through your classified telephone directory and making a list of service organizations, hospitals, churches, and clubs. Get in touch with the ones that interest you and ask about their needs for the summer. At the same time watch news items in local papers. They'll also give you leads.

Your first volunteer job as a teenager may not prove to be a ticket to your future, but that happy possibility does exist—and service is the rent you pay for the space you occupy in the world!

Volunteer work, however, need not be the kind of service you limit only to summers, since many teenagers do it in their free time all year 'round.

Two teenagers who make the most of their free time are two sisters from Flushing, New York, who work as candy-stripers in the Salvation Army's Booth Memorial Hospital in Flushing, New York.

Although their mother works full time and after school they're involved with the care of their four younger brothers and sisters at home, they find time to do their volunteer work as a team, between them contributing two full days a week to the hospital during the summer and a whole day every Saturday while school is in session. While one sister takes care of the young children at home during the morning, the other one checks into the hospital volunteer office for their joint day's work in Emergency where they register incoming patients, escort them to X-ray and do whatever tasks are asked of them. In the afternoon the girls switch jobs. With all the demands upon their time at home, the sisters are among the most faithful candystripers at Booth.

Here are some of the many advantages to volunteer work:

- It helps you grow into a mature person who accepts adult responsibilities.
- It provides experience in getting along with people.
- It gives you "social responsibility"—another term for paying the rent for the space you occupy.
- It fosters good work habits, and provides useful experiences and character references that may be helpful when you're looking for a paying job.
- It gives the satisfaction of knowing that you are useful. Once you've had the experiences of seeing how much you're needed, you'll look forward eagerly to the next volunteer job!

Under the leadership of the Red Cross, a group of Riverside, California, high school students "adopted" fifty teenage patients at the Patton State Hospital in San Bernardino, almost singlehandedly supporting the needs of a school program at the hospital.

When the hospital took its plunge into an education program for its teenage patients, the Riverside High School Red Cross helpers entered the picture, and the young volunteers began to gather textbooks and school supplies for the hospital's school. Next, they obtained a record player, hundreds of records, magazines, and sports equipment.

Even after the hospital's school budget problem was solved, there seemed to be something missing, so a meeting of young patients with the Riverside teens was arranged to find out what the patients' wants and needs were. Basically, they proved to be the same as those of every teenager. They wanted parties, mail, and ways to meet new people!

Since that time the Riverside teen volunteers have tried to fill these needs by putting on a dance at the hospital on most major holidays. Before the first one, held at Christmas in 1962, the Riverside teens did a lot of worrying. What should they wear, what could they talk about—and would the venture be a blast or a frost?

But at the end of the highly successful dance all of the teens had but one thing to ask: "When do we have another one?"

Volunteer work gives you a made-to-order chance to explore job and career opportunities in such fields as health, education, politics, and social work. At the same time, it gives you an excellent chance to test your abilities and interests in real situations and provides you with some of the best opportunities you'll ever have to learn whether your current interest in a job field is something you want to follow or whether you should look elsewhere for a career.

As one high school Senior put it, "Volunteer work in our hospital ended up deciding me against nursing as a career. But I gained a great deal from it, anyhow, because it encouraged me to work with people and help them in other situations besides nursing. I did enjoy helping people who needed help."

In addition to the types of work we've already mentioned there are many other volunteer projects to which young people can contribute.

Collecting Money

Collecting money for service organizations is an important job, and the effects of it can be far-reaching, too, as Paulette Breen, a former "Miss American Teen-Ager" found out when she spent her year's reign spearheading nationwide teenage campaigns in behalf of UNICEF and other organizations.

In one snow-covered Alaskan village, teenagers under her leadership divided the area into three sections and traveled by boat to outlying districts (since they had no automobiles in their small fishing village), spreading the word of the UNICEF project for children who lack sufficient food, medical care and education. Hawaiian teens gave up their surfboarding to plan a UNICEF Halloween at Maui, gathering together the members of the fifteen Y Clubs and other village youth for their program.

In Wyoming, one teenage girl worked all by herself one Halloween because she wanted to do something to show her concern for the other people of the world, but her enthusiasm was so contagious that the next year more young people joined her in the project she'd started alone.

Working for Senior Citizens

Shopping for shut-ins, visiting old peoples' homes or working in some other way to fill the needs of senior citizens is a volunteer opportunity many teenagers find rewarding.

A West Virginia chapter of the Future Homemakers of America, for example, adopted fifteen senior citizens of their community and then visited them throughout the year, sent them cards and letters, and cooked special dishes for them. Another chapter assigned members in pairs to visit regularly thirty-nine older people in the community. In one town the service projects for the year included home visiting, sending cards, Christmas caroling, providing flower arrangements, wrapping gifts, mailing cards and packages, running errands, and staying with older people at night.

The young volunteers deepened their appreciation for peoples' needs by asking the older people to teach them such things as ceramics, flower and vegetable gardening, flower arranging, needlepointing, drapery-making and other skills. One group organized a Grandad Club, which in turn helped the young people tile their school's food laboratory as a special project.

Political Work

Working for the political party of your choice is another kind of teenage volunteer job well worth thinking about. Often this work can lead to political careers, because a person acquires both contacts and background while serving as a volunteer. Young volunteers in both parties do such varied jobs as addressing, stuffing, sealing and stamping envelopes; typing letters; mimeographing statements and press releases; filing in campaign headquarters; driving cars or sound trucks broadcasting political messages; ringing doorbells to urge people to register or vote; helping to fill large halls or auditoriums where candidates are to speak; helping to organize meetings, rallies, and demonstrations; manning telephones in telephone campaigns; making campaign signs and carrying them; distributing campaign literature; baby-sitting on election day; chauffeuring people to and from the polls on election day; organizing fund-raising projects.

Both Republicans and Democrats provide special programs to help teenagers learn about the party. Teenage volunteers learn how to organize their own discussion sessions and forums at which national leaders speak.

The Republican party has the welcome mat out for volunteer workers with its teenage organization TARS. The Democratic party does the same with its Teen Dem program.

Working with Handicapped Children

Working with handicapped or retarded children is another volunteer project in which teenagers can be of great
service.

The boys and girls of one high school service group
make it their business to escort blind children to bowling
parties. On other occasions they play ball with mentally
retarded children. The teenagers often make a point of
being the losers so that the children can know what it's
like to win.

There is a group of Red Cross teens serving regularly at
the Stockley Hospital for the Mentally Retarded in southern Delaware, where they play games both indoors and
outdoors with the young patients, read stories to them,
and sometimes just rock and love them. Although such
work is hard and demanding, these young people praise
it for all the rewards it gives them in the love and affec-
tion of their small charges.

Club Work

One of the most popular kinds of volunteer work for
young people all over the country is participating in the
service projects of Y's, boys' and girls' clubs, Campfire
Girls, Scouts, neighborhood centers, settlement houses, or
church youth groups.

One group of Hi-Y and Tri-Hi-Y Clubs of the Northeast
Branch of the Sacramento, California, YMCA completed
what they believe to be a "first" in the Hi-Y Movement
when they followed through on their idea to build a
chapel for the YMCA.

After three years of countless candy sales, bake sales,
car washes, dances, newspaper and bottle collections and
other fund-raising activities, the young workers had raised
$7,000—about half of what was needed. After that, they

went to work securing gifts of materials and labor so that their $7,000 would do the job.

As a result of their soliciting, the concrete was donated. Next the lumber was secured for $200 below the dealer's cost. After that the glass was donated. Then came $1,700 worth of labor. As the donations rolled in, the teenagers rolled up their sleeves and went to work, digging the foundations, hanging sheet rock and painting walls.

It took them four months to construct the chapel. But when it was done it stood there proudly—a $15,000 building for club inductions, officer installations, weekly Hi-Y religious programs, weddings, and special seasonal programs. In addition, a congregation that has no church building meets there every Sunday.

Still other projects that can be handled by volunteer teenagers are community clean-up and improvement jobs.

For example, one group of Key Clubbers, a service club for high school boys sponsored by Kiwanis International, scoured the town of Fox Valley, Georgia, for abandoned refrigerators—treacherous hiding places for small children who know no better than to creep inside an empty box and shut the door.

To prevent this danger in their town, the Key Clubbers divided the city into four districts. Then three or four club members were assigned to canvass each district and persuade owners to remove the danger to children by taking locks off their old ice boxes.

In conjunction with the canvass, the teenagers obtained coverage in the local newspaper, along with spots on every radio newscast for three days. Several club members also printed circulars that were distributed throughout the city. Hazardous conditions were remedied in several cases.

Fortunately, you don't have to have a specific talent to get a job as a volunteer worker! In most cases, you don't have to know a great deal about the job when you volunteer, either, because you learn by doing. In many volunteer jobs you receive special training.

On the whole, the best way to get a volunteer job is to look around your town for groups and clubs doing what interests you, and then offer your services.

If you prefer a volunteer job where you'll work on your own instead of with a group, you can find such work by applying at the local office of any national service organization or by talking with community-minded people in your town and volunteering your time.

Once you decide to commit yourself to some kind of volunteer project, make up your mind to succeed at the job by doing four things:

1. Match your volunteer job to your own talent and interests and make sure you believe in it wholeheartedly.

2. Before signing up for a volunteer job make a serious analysis of how much time you'll have for the work. Plan before you take the plunge. But once you say you'll take the job, be as dependable in it as you would be on a paying job.

3. Unless you have lots of hours to give to volunteer activities, resolve to do an active and good job for one or two organizations rather than be an inactive member with your name on the roll call of innumerable ones. It's much better to be present at one job than it is to be absent from ten!

4. Wherever you work as a volunteer, make a genuine effort to get along with other workers. You'll meet all types in volunteer jobs, so when things don't always go right remember that errors are human, while forgiveness is divine.

If you succeed in doing these things you'll be paying for

your space on earth, and like a girl describing her job working with brain-damaged children, you'll be able to say, "I feel good inside!"

16

Hold Everything—
with Personality Plus

PERSONALITY has been described as the length of the shadow that you can cast on a job or future.

Job-wise, that hits the nail on the head, because in most cases the personality you show each day makes people like or dislike you and decides how far you will go. A number of surveys show that of all the people who lose their jobs only ten per cent of them lose out because they lack the ability required. The other ninety per cent fail because of undesirable personality traits! That alone is adequate proof that as you plan for your future you will need to consider (1) what makes people like and admire a personality, (2) and how you can develop that kind of popularity-plus yourself.

What Personality Traits Do Your Friends Admire?

In a survey of traits considered most conducive to success by young people, the following ones got all the votes

as the measuring rods teenagers would use to pick out the
person "most popular" and "most likely to succeed":

1. A helpful and cheerful attitude
2. Tact and diplomacy
3. Respect for people's feelings
4. Good moral standards
5. A sense of humor and the ability to laugh easily
6. All-around friendliness combined with a ready smile
7. Tolerance of other people's faults
8. Honesty
9. Good sportsmanship
10. The courage to stand up and speak up for the things you believe in
11. Determination
12. Kindness and understanding
13. Patience
14. Good manners
15. Consideration for other people
16. Independence
17. Self-control
18. Perseverance
19. Humbleness
20. Ambition

What Personality Traits Do Employers Like?

Employers from many towns and cities, when asked to list
the personality traits they liked in young employees as
well as the qualities that rate for getting ahead, included
the ones on the following list. Many of them repeat what
the teens selected, so start to develop all these good traits
now. You'll use them all your life.

1. A respect for customers, fellow employees and supervisors
2. A willingness to do the job required with a cheerful and pleasant attitude, no matter how little or unimportant it seems
3. A tactful, suggestive approach when presenting opposing views to supervisory people
4. Ability to get along with people
5. A strong determination to do one's best at a job
6. Good grooming

7. Honesty and integrity
8. Punctuality
9. Courtesy, politeness and good manners
10. An interest in the work and a genuine desire to please
11. An open mind that shows an eagerness to learn
12. A love of work
13. A constant display of effort
14. Consideration for other people
15. Cooperation
16. Humility
17. Dependability
18. A willingness to listen
19. Perseverance
20. Loyalty
21. The ability to speak well and communicate well with others
22. Drive and initiative
23. Accuracy and neatness
24. Enthusiasm
25. Intelligence, training, and skill
26. Alertness
27. Reverence for achievement
28. Tolerance and understanding of human frailties

Attitudes Employers Don't Like

Employers gave the following traits a "no future" rating when it came to getting ahead. Try to eliminate these undesirable characteristics if you feel they threaten your career.

"SEE YOURSELF" JOB APTITUDE TEST

Tardiness
Disrespect
Laziness
Argumentative disposition

Superior attitude toward fellow employees and employers

Poor attendance and absence without notification

Unwillingness to start at the bottom

Accepting as rights what are really privileges

Sloppiness in grooming

Arrogance

Inattentiveness and carelessness

An "I-don't care" attitude

Irresponsibility

Lack of appreciation for pay scale

"Chip-on-the-shoulder" attiude

The "What-can-you-do-for-me?" approach

Disclosure of private company data

Dishonesty and misrepresentation

Now it's time for a thorough check-up on fifty important personality points. Some are plus points we've mentioned. Others are something else. But together they spell "popularity plus" and make people like and admire you for all the things you are.

If you have your share of the total, you're popular all the time—with boys, with girls, in jobs, at school, and everywhere you go. Answer each question truthfully. On a piece of scrap paper write "yes" or "no" beside each number.

You needn't complete the quiz all at once. Take plenty of time to think. Then, when you reach the fifty-yard line, tally up your score.

SEE YOURSELF QUIZ FOR POPULARITY PLUS

1. Do you restrain yourself from complaining and do the best you can with what you have?

2. Do you realize that constructive criticism is often given to you to help you?

3. Do you put quality and good workmanship into all your jobs and projects?

4. Do you act mature instead of childish?

5. Do you accept people for what they are and appreciate their good points rather than their weaknesses?

6. Are you kind and friendly to everyone?

7. Are you an interesting person because you involve yourself with a big variety of interests outside of yourself?

8. Do you have a reputation for being happy and cheerful?

9. Do you allow your good feelings for people to show? For instance, when you like people do you show it? And when you're sympathetic do you show that, too?

10. Are you a good conversationalist because you read good books, keep up on current events and—along with your favorite pop singers—listen to stimulating programs on radio and television?

11. Do you try to improve your speaking voice by reading aloud, listening to yourself on a tape recorder, and attempting to learn from people whose quality of speech is good?

12. Are you courteous instead of discourteous under all circumstances?

13. Do you show that you care about other people's needs?

14. Do you always say "Thank you," "Please," and "Excuse me"?

15. Do you give compliments when they're deserved?

16. Do you make the most of your looks?

17. Do you get fun out of life?

18. Do you refrain from speaking to older people or your boss as informally as you speak to your best friend?

19. Do you knock on a door and wait for "Come in" before entering a room if a door happens to be closed?

20. Do you practice good telephone manners by answer-

ing the phone graciously instead of brusquely and by hanging up the phone gently after you've said good-bye?

21. Can you write letters in a natural, friendly style and keep them clear and brief?

22. Have you a sense of humor and the ability to laugh at yourself?

23. Do you smile and speak to people when you're the person who has to speak first?

24. Do you act lively instead of bored?

25. Do you learn all you can about a job while you have it so that the background and experience from that job can be used for getting ahead later on?

26. Are you trying to develop that rare and wonderful knack of making everything you do seem like the most important thing you have to do that day?

27. Similarly, can you make people feel important?

28. Do you avoid self-pity?

29. Do you steer yourself away from being supersensitive about everything that happens to you?

30. Do you avoid the bad habit of constantly sighing out loud?

31. Are you optimistic rather than pessimistic?

32. Are you willing to listen to both sides of a story in the belief that your opinions are not always superior to other people's?

33. Do you accept some challenges instead of always asking, "What if this should happen?"

34. Do you talk more about the promise of the future than the failures of the past?

35. Are you flexible and adaptable to new ideas and changes as they come along?

36. Do you avoid saying thoughtless things that prick with the sharpness of a pin?

37. Do you avoid talking about being tired all the time?

38. Do you prove by your actions as well as your words that you're ready and willing to assume responsibilty?
39. Are you enthusiastic about life in general?
40. Have you proved to people that you're dependable?
41. Are you always willing to do your share of the work without grousing and griping?
42. Do you try to make an effort to be generous instead of selfish?
43. Do you show some initiative instead of letting other people do your thinking?
44. Do you keep away from gossip, regardless of how tempting and juicy it is?
45. Do you know when to speak and when to keep quiet?
46. Do you refrain from arguing too much?
47. Do you check yourself regularly for annoying personal habits such as sniffling, loud gum chewing, or too much throat clearing?
48. Are you creating your own opportunities to do more than what is asked of you so that people see all the things you can do?
49. Have you made a wise decision in the matter of teen-age drinking?
50. Are you tying your personality together with a strong set of values and high ideals?

What's Your Score?

When you finish this soul-searching session on personality plus, total the number of Yes's to figure out your score.

If the number totals 50 you're too good to be true. In fact, if it hits 40 you have personality plus! If you balance the scales between 30 and 40, you're still quite personable. And even when you hit 25 there's a good chance that people like you.

But if you're under that figure you need to get on the

ball and start developing some of the traits you need to get ahead.

Here are a few for your start.

How to Improve

Your Appearance

> DO make an effort to dress well
> DON'T be colorless and drab
> DO groom yourself till you shine with cleanliness
> DON'T settle for being sloppy
> DO be the master of your weight
> DON'T let your weight master you

Your Attitude toward Yourself

> DO build a fire under yourself and show some spark and sparkle
> DON'T go through your days and weeks as though you're serving time
> DO develop self-confidence
> DON'T depend on others to do what you can do
> DO work to get the best things in life
> DON'T settle for second best

Your Attitude toward Others

> DO pay attention to people
> DON'T be standoffish and diffident
> DO be considerate of others
> DON'T think of yourself above all else
> DO realize other people know a few things too
> DON'T think you know it all yourself

Your Relationship with Others

> DO practice the art of forgiveness
> DON'T hold a grudge forever
> DO learn to converse with people
> DON'T lapse into nonstop silences
> DO admit it when you're wrong
> DON'T always have to be right

Your Approach to School or Jobs
>   DO try to do your best every day
>   DON'T give up before you start
>   DO look for opportunities
>   DON'T wait for them to come first
>   DO show you're interested in your work
>   DON'T make it clear that you're bored

17

Use of Your Money and Time

"I NEVER HAVE enough money" and "I never have enough time" are two frequent teen complaints. Money problems fall into one of three variations: "I can't earn enough," "I can't keep enough," or "I can never save enough."

This is true of teen time to a lesser degree. Some young people manage miraculously to get many things done.

Others, however, bemoan the fact that time slips away from them. One boy commented honestly, "I spend more time wondering where I'll find time to do things than I spend getting anything done."

Both time and money are vital to your future, so let's see what you're doing with your share of both of them.

Where Do Teens Get Their Money?

If you're like most young people around the country you get your money from more than one source.

According to a "Study of the Youth Market" conducted by Scholastic Magazines, a cross section of young people in seventh grade through twelfth reported that they received their money from the following sources:

49%—Regular allowance
48%—Earned part-time outside home
33%—Received odd amounts from parents
18%—Earned doing special jobs at home

More than half of the students reported more than one source of income.

How Much Do Teens Get Each Week?

Surveys differ on the total amount teenagers accumulate each week. But the Scholastic Magazines study reported above shows the average amount of income received by junior and senior high school students to be as follows:

$ 6.77—average over-all
   4.89—   ″   for Junior H.S. boys
   3.88—   ″   ″   ″   ″   girls
  11.67—   ″   ″ Senior ″   boys
   7.24—   ″   ″   ″   ″   girls

On the other hand, a study covering more than 12,000 city and rural children made by the Eugene Gilbert Company showed that, on the average, student allowances range between $5 and $6 for the majority of teenage boys and between $3 and $4 for girls.

What Do Teens Do with Their Money?

Strictly from the girls' point of view, a survey conducted in four southern states of forty state officers of the Future Homemakers of America shows that the income received by this particular group of young people goes for church, gifts for the family, and spending money for movies, bowling, skating, records, and magazines.

When the survey got around to the matter of savings, though, none of the girls surveyed was entirely pleased with her record. More than half of the girls reported inability to save as their major problem in money management. Half said they saved "sometimes." One commented, "I can't save a broken dollar. Once it becomes change, it's gone."

Still another girl stated that her inability to save stemmed from her inability to determine what's a necessity and what's a luxury. All the girls believed in saving money, however, because when asked what they would do with a sudden windfall of $25, more than half of them answered that they'd put it in savings accounts.

The Scholastic Magazines study, covering both boys and girls, shows that 72% of the young people interviewed reported that they saved some of the money they received.

The following table shows a comparison of the average amount saved by all who received money during one week (some saved more) with the average amount received by this same group. It shows that about half of the money received was saved:

	All Students	Junior H.S. Boys	Junior H.S. Girls	Senior H.S. Boys	Senior H.S. Girls
Average Received	$6.77	$4.89	$3.88	$11.67	$7.24
Average Saved	3.33	2.61	1.68	6.04	3.45
% Saved	49%	51%	45%	52%	48%

Where Do Teens Keep Their Money?

According to the same survey, places used for saving money were reported as follows:

68%—Home (in a bank or special place)
51%—Bank Account (commercial or savings)
15%—Savings and Loan Association
15%—U. S. Savings Stamps or Bonds
8%—Christmas or Vacation Club
7%—Insurance

For What Purpose Do Teens Save Money?

In the Scholastic Magazines survey young people listed the following as their most important reasons for saving:

29% for education
18% for clothes
10% for a car
6% for sports equipment
1% each for photographic equipment, portable radio, typewriter
26% for no special item

What's the Best Way to Handle Money?

For lots of us, learning to handle money is a lifetime effort and challenge. Most of us never have enough, and we never save enough either!

But all of us do much better by working out sensible plans.

Money won't buy happiness or the blessings of friends and love. But provided it's not an obsession that ends up being a sort of god, it will give you many good things in life. For example, it gives you

1. a financial backlog to use when opportunities knock
2. a feeling of self-reliance and independence
3. a wonderful sense of security and peace of mind that comes of knowing that you have provided for unexpected crises

How Can You Manage Money Instead of Letting It Manage You?

One of the really practical ways to save is to save a dime from each dollar, beginning with the next dollar that comes into your hand!

When you squeeze out a dime from that dollar, put it away in your piggy bank till you're ready to stash it away in your local bank. You'll see the money accumulate with a speed you'd never expect.

According to figures provided by the National Thrift Committee, here are the amounts you can have twenty years from today if you start saving now:

SAVINGS ACCUMULATED OVER A PERIOD OF TWENTY YEARS

Amount Saved Per Month	1 yr.	5 yrs.	10 yrs.	15 yrs.	20 yrs.
$ 1.00	$ 12.00	$ 60.00	$ 120.00	$ 180.00	$ 240.00
5.00	60.00	300.00	600.00	900.00	1200.00
10.00	120.00	600.00	1200.00	1800.00	2400.00
25.00	300.00	1500.00	3000.00	4500.00	6000.00

Note: Earnings added and compounded will increase the totals outlined in this chart.

Other Ways to Manage Money

Use as your guide some of the many booklets purposely prepared to help young people learn to handle money. The titles of three of them follow, and each includes a discussion of budgets and ways to make them work.

"Teens' Guide to Money Management." Released by the National Thrift Committee, Inc., 121 West Wacker Drive, Chicago, Ill. 60601.

"A Miss and Her Money." Released by Women's Division, Institute of Life Insurance, 277 Park Avenue, New York, N.Y. 10017.

"Why Go Broke?" Released by Institute of Life Insurance, 277 Park Avenue, New York, N.Y. 10017.

What About Your Bank of Time?

Now that we've thought about money and banks, let's look at your bank of time.

You do have a time bank, if you look at this priceless commodity from the viewpoint that everyone in the world has the same twenty-four hours a day! The total number of minutes is 1440. Some of us use it wisely, but others while it away, saying, "If only I had the time to do what I want to do!"

You can find the time if you will organize your days and weeks so that you use it instead of losing it.

Here are some tips for salvaging idle minutes.

Pop Out of Bed in the Morning

If you're a person whose first word is "No!" when you hear the alarm clock ring, this method of using and saving time may not be the tip you've been waiting for all the days of your life. But it's a tip that has worked mighty well for lots of people who have built for themselves the best in jobs and futures.

"Long ago I learned one method that saves me anywhere from twenty to fifty minutes daily," TV star Arthur Godfrey reported on one occasion.

The method? When he wakes up, he simply gets right up. As far as he's concerned, lingering in bed only delays the inevitable!

Organize Your Day

Another person who has practiced good habits through a very famous career is ex-President of the United States General Dwight D. Eisenhower. He shortens his morning dressing time by setting everything out the night before, and then he reflects his West Point training by lining up all the next day's equipment so it will be close at hand.

You can give your day this same good start by keeping your clothes in good order and by lining up at night all the things you'll need for the next day. Keep on your desk, bureau, or some other easily accessible spot the things you use every day. Then you won't waste precious time looking for keys, glasses, pencils, pens and all the other miscellaneous items that make you lose minutes while you turn your pockets inside out.

Before you close your eyes for the night, list in your mind or on paper the things you have to do and the things you want to do for the next twenty-four hours. During those twenty-four hours you may have to be flexible and switch your plans around a bit. But knowing in advance what you'd like to do and what you have to do gives you a goal for each day and shows you what you must do and what you can leave out, should the need arise. As you accomplish things, it's satisfying to cross them off a list.

SPECIAL TIMESAVERS FOR EACH DAY

1. Instead of wasting unexpected spare time waiting for people or appointments, always have something with you to read or study.
2. Generally speaking, do one thing at a time and stick to that until you finish it.
3. Learn to be selective about your activities. Say no to commitments that have no important meaning for anyone and no real interest for you.

What Will You Do with the Time You Save?

There's not much point in saving time in one place to fritter away somewhere else, so use those extra minutes for activities that are meaningful for you. An old book published in 1891, *Successful Life,* expressed the idea very well:

"Every man wastes more than time enough to make him famous. Half an hour a day saved from the wasted moments of your life and devoted to any field of inquiry will make you master of it in a dozen years."

18

Follow the Lead
of Those Who Succeed

THE purpose of this book has been to show you how to make the most of your journey into your future by suggesting (1) how other people have done it and (2) what you can do for yourself.

If you've kept your "See Yourself" notebook, you've written down your goals, and this will help you, because, when you run into disappointments and need to switch direction, the fact that you know where you're going is on your side all the while. With perseverance, imagination and enthusiasm, chances are you'll reach your goal.

Dancer Leslie Gearhart, who realized her ambition of being a full-fledged ballerina with a major dance company by the time she was seventeen, had decided when she was ten that she wanted a career in the dance field. From that time on, her image of herself never changed and she never once lost sight of her goal to be a successful ballerina.

To show her parents how serious she was, even when she was ten, she practiced her dancing lessons at home in all her spare time and trained hard at a bar set in an alcove in her bedroom. In every way she worked so hard to reach her goal that by the time she was fourteen she was accepted at the Washington School of Ballet. From that day on, she enured herself to a kind of sacrifice unknown to many teenagers.

To keep up with everything while going to high school her schedule demanded early rising and working until late at night. Since she lived in Virginia, she usually did homework en route to her dancing classes in Washington. In order to finish high school and launch her career more quickly, she accelerated her school work by taking more courses than required and by attending summer school.

After a stint of working at this high-pressure pace, Leslie narrowed down to a 9 A.M. to 9 P.M. schedule by enrolling in the academic program sponsored by the dancing school. In this way she could combine her dance lessons with her high school work.

When Leslie became a full-fledged member of the Washington Ballet, sacrifice continued to be the order of the day as she rehearsed with the company all week, had classes on Saturday morning and rehearsed from 4 to 6 Saturday afternoons. Sometimes she rehearsed on Sunday, too, so her only free time was Saturday evening.

But sacrifice paved the way to success. Several months after she received her high school diploma, Leslie won a place in the Harkness Ballet, the newest major ballet company in America.

Your own goal may not be dancing. But if you've kept your "See Yourself" notebook, you can run through the goals that you wrote down at the start of this book. Then check the notes you've written and finish up with a final "See Yourself" evaluation chart like the one outlined below. Allow plenty of space in your notebook for this final check list.

"SEE-YOURSELF" QUIZ FOR RE-EVALUATION
OF MY PRESENT AND FUTURE IMAGE AND GOALS

	WHERE I STAND NOW	WHERE I HOPE TO STAND IN TEN YEARS	HOW I PLAN TO GET THERE
Education			
Achievements			
Personality			
Interests			
Abilities			

Regardless of the plans you will write on your final "See Yourself" chart, here are ten final tickets for that future you are building.

Ticket 1
Be willing to take the time that it takes to succeed

Here's a tip just for you from TV star Bud Collyer:

"When you're a young person seeking a career, remember that the world doesn't owe you a living or a good career. If you're going to make the grade, you have to prepare yourself to take the time the career will take. And while you're taking the time you can't ever acknowledge the words 'give up.'

"I learned this lesson at Williams College. It happened while I was in a lab studying a slide one day and watching a paramecium struggling to get a piece of hair. For a long time the paramecium couldn't make it. But it wouldn't give up its goal and eventually it got the hair.

"That made a great impression on me, and I decided then and there that if that tiny form of life with no intelligence can keep trying and make the grade, certainly we human beings ought to be able to make the grade, too!"

Ticket 2

Enjoy what you do every day

We become what we are by many separate, seemingly insignificant acts, so reaching a goal is a daily thing that should give us satisfaction as we go. It's your life you're spending, and it's important to be just as excited and contented while you're traveling toward your goal as you expect to be when you get there. The journey, as many of the successful have found, can often be as glorious as the pot of gold at the end of it.

Madame Marie Curie, discoverer of radium, said many times that the happiest years of her life were spent, not after the great discovery, but during the four years that she and her husband worked in an old shed, with no money and no other help, trying and trying to extract one decigram of pure radium from their truckload of pitchblende.

Ticket 3

Have the courage to be yourself

Once you see yourself as the person you want to become, have the courage to be that person and pay the price of becoming that person.

Metropolitan opera singer Roberta Peters in talking to teens in *Seventeen* magazine points out how difficult it is during your teens to be different from your crowd and to be an individual who does what he or she knows must be done to achieve a goal.

"It's always a lot easier to join them, to do what they do, to think their way," she writes. "But if there is something you want and have to do, there comes a time when you must go it alone."

To achieve what she wanted to do, Roberta Peters "went it alone" many times. She paid the price of the success she wanted by concentrating completely on her musical studies. But the price she paid won her her goal.

Ticket 4

Be a good friend to yourself, and like yourself

It's so easy to give up on yourself when you see your own imperfections! But when you're ready to throw in the sponge because you feel so imperfect, remember that no one is perfect and that the greatest work of the world is done by imperfect people.

Don't sell yourself short because of your own imperfections. Instead, decide to accept yourself for the person you can be.

"Sometimes I have been able to help young people most importantly," Lucille Ball has said, "by making them acknowledge what they find good about themselves. I find that as soon as they actually are made to acknowledge the good things, they can almost instantly begin to like themselves a little better."

Ticket 5

Realize that you often have to fail before you succeed

Many young people worry unduly about mistakes and failures! Nobody likes to fail, of course. But mistakes are part of growing up, and you can learn and profit from them if you turn them into lessons, chalk them up to experience and start all over again to prove what you can do. Most great people have failed now and then on their way to the top, and most of them, when you ask them, willingly attest to this fact.

While Katherine Cornell, that great lady of the American stage, was still in school, her acting in a school play came to the attention of Edward Goodman of the Washington Square Players, and when he saw her act he told her if she ever considered the theater as a career she should come to see him.

Consequently, when Katherine Cornell left the girls' school she attended, she moved to New York and went to Edward Goodman's office. Although he didn't recognize her at first, he did agree to give her a chance to read a part.

Once on stage, however, Katherine was filled with fear. She was afraid she wasn't pretty enough. Her poise completely disappeared and her performance was ineffective.

When she heard Mr. Goodman keep calling, "Louder!" she knew how badly she was missing. Then, feeling like a failure, she gave up, left the stage, ran out of the theater, and walked blindly up the street.

It wasn't easy to regain her confidence in her ability to do what she really wanted to do after that. And it wasn't easy to keep telling herself that she must chalk up the failure to experience and try again.

But, instead of scrapping all her hopes, Katherine Cornell determined that she would work tirelessly to become the great actress she ultimately was.

Ticket 6

*Be earnest about your goals,
but don't take yourself so seriously
that you can't accept a bad performance
now and then*

Instead of working up into a fret over every activity of the day that goes wrong, accept the fact that each new day presents a new chance.

Comedian Jack Benny once said that when he was very young—really thirty-nine!—he drove himself slowly crazy fuming about every bad day he had, even if his work for the day had been adequate. He took himself so seriously that he thought he was going to have a nervous breakdown each time he went on the air, because he wanted his show to be so perfect.

But now he looks at things differently. When you work hard and do the best you can, he believes, everything seems to work out.

Ticket 7

Surround yourself with
many worthwhile interests
while you concentrate on a main interest

Concert pianist Hilde Somer, who concentrated on her goal of succeeding as a pianist from the time that she was twelve, is one successful person who is so in love with life that she can't point out too emphatically the value of having many interests.

"In my frequent and intimate contact with teenagers as a teacher, lecturer, and concert pianist, I feel very strongly about the inspiring and stimulating value of having many interests," she said in an interview. "And the teenagers I know who are the most interested and most fulfilled ones are the young people who are active in many fields outside their set programs.

"I myself am deeply grateful to have had influences that catapulted me into a multitude of interests. It helps me in every phase of my life—in being a musician, a wife and mother, in writing or TV work, and in my relationship to the world.

"Agonizing boredom and lost souls would be dying

out," she concluded, "if people had more interests and involvements with all the great things the world puts within our reach."

Ticket 8

Believe in yourself to the point where you're willing to work hard and prepare for an opportunity you may never get

When you're serious about building a good future, you have to look ahead and prepare yourself for the kind of chance you can't see on your present horizon.

Arlene Francis is quick to point out the tremendous need in everyone's life to be prepared for the next step and the next opportunity.

"Earlier in my own career," she has said, "I observed that the people who were getting the most parts on the stage were the ones who were the most versatile. Consequently, I began studying accents to improve my versatility.

"If this kind of studying meant that I had to go see a movie twenty-one times in order to observe and learn an accent, I went twenty-one times. I also went to see almost every foreign actress performing in New York. Then I'd go home and read Shakespeare with different accents."

Arlene's preparation for opportunities before they arrived did pay off. There was a role in a Broadway play for a girl with a Russian accent, and hers sounded so genuine that she got the part.

Ticket 9

Keep believing in yourself, and learn to conquer disappointment

Disappointments always hurt, but they come to everyone. When you have them—and you'll have your share—refuse to let them crush your spirit. Instead, keep building for what you want in spite of career disappointments.

If all people let disappointments smother their ambitions and crush their spirits the world would miss a great many valuable things. According to one news story, disappointments were very often the order of the day before Mary Martin got her first real break. But she never lost her special brand of sparkle and her belief that she could become what she wanted to be. As a result, when a new singer with a special style was needed for a new song in a new show, Mary was on hand to take the opportunity when it was offered to her. And when the curtain went down on her first performance of the song "My Heart Belongs to Daddy," the rest of her career became history.

Ticket 10

When you're prepared for a job or career,
plan to go where the jobs are and take almost
any starting job in your field of interest

A job "opportunity" is sometimes described as being at the right place at the right time with the right thing to offer to the right person. Many people testify to this in interviews.

Skitch Henderson has a multiple career as composer, conductor, orchestra leader, pianist, recording artist, and concert and television personality. "I believe young people have to go where big things are going on right in the beginning of their careers," says Skitch. "If you don't, you won't compete above your own level. Neither will you give yourself the opportunity to be on hand should a good chance arise."

To show how this worked out in his career, Skitch tells the story of one of his own early jobs in a parking lot in Hollywood. At that time, he'd graduated from college, was practicing the piano constantly and was getting further specialized training for the career he wanted. But to be near the top movie studios where a lot was going on, he took the job in the parking lot.

"When one day the studio needed a rehearsal pianist quickly to play mood music for a star," Skitch Henderson says, "I was available, so I got my chance.

"After that, a lot of other things began to happen— which is why I believe in taking almost any job in the beginning if it's close to the area in which you hope to achieve success."

What Is Success?

Success has been mentioned many times in this book, but what do we mean by success?

Success wears many smiles. To some of your friends it means the biggest swimming pool in town, or maybe the most expensive sports car, or the largest assortment of clothes. To others it may mean full wallets, or a job that people envy because it looks so good. But these are only outer signs. Real success is within. It's never what you do or have. Instead, it's what you are!

We hope success will smile on you. That's the reason for this book. But the best smile is your smile that means happiness inside, because (1) you have a genuine purpose and goal and know where you're going, (2) you're involved in work to which every day you give the best you can offer, and (3) you enjoy the work you do every day and see meaning in your daily achievement.

Those feelings are better than anything that the money from any job buys. So be true to yourself and become inside the person you yourself can admire, whether you make your living as a banker or a baker, a teacher or a technician, a scientist or a stenographer, a philosopher or a plumber.

Time and maturity will be on your side, but now you can write your own ticket to being what you want to be. You can't be an expert in everything, and you can't be all things to all people. But you can build your job and your future in a world that has never been so full of so many things to do.

You won't achieve your goals overnight. But you will achieve them by trying—and by believing in your ability and in a God who is good.

In the words attributed to Aldous Huxley, "Every man who knows how to read has it in his power to magnify himself, to multiply the ways in which he exists, to make his life full, significant and interesting." This is a message for all of you, as you build your own job and future!

Blessings, and luck to you!

Suggested Reading List
for Students

The following books, booklets and pamphlets have been especially chosen for further reading because of their application to the subject of this book:

BOOKS

Andersen, S. Katz, M., and Shimberg, B., *Meeting the Test*. New York, N. Y., Scholastic Book Services, 1964.

Bowles, Frank H., *How to Get Into College*. New York, N. Y., E. P. Dutton & Co., 1958.

Boynton, Paul W., *6 Ways to Get a Job*. New York, N. Y., Harper & Row, 1951.

Brand, Ira, *100 Proven Ways to Boost Your Campus Income*. New York, N. Y., Brand Books, 1964.

Cox, Claire, *How to Beat the High Cost of College*. New York, N. Y., Bernard Geis Associates, 1964.

Edlund, S. W., and M. G., *Pick Your Job and Land It*. Englewood Cliffs, N. J., Prentice-Hall, Inc., 1954.

Gruber, Edward C., *Résumés That Get Jobs*. New York, N.Y., Arco Publishing Co., 1963.

Hartogs, Dr. Renatus, and Fletcher, Helen Jill, *How to Grow Up Successfully*. Indianapolis, Indiana, The Bobbs-Merrill Co., Inc., 1961.

Haupt, Enid A., *The Seventeen Book of Young Living*. New York, N. Y.. David McKay Co., Inc., 1957.

Hoopes, Ray, *The Complete Peace Corps Guide*. New York, N. Y., The Dial Press, Inc., 1961.

King, Alice Gore, *Career Opportunities for Women in Business*. New York, N. Y., E. P. Dutton & Co., 1963.

O'Sullivan, Joan, *100 Ways to Popularity*. New York, N. Y., The Macmillan Company, 1963.

Peake, Miriam Morrison, *101 Things to Make for Fun or Money*. New York, N. Y. Scholastic Book Services, 1964.

Sulkin, Sidney, *Complete Planning for College*. New York, N. Y., McGraw-Hill Book Co., 1964.

Willing, Jules Z., *How to Land the Job You Want,* New York, N. Y., Signet Key Book, New American Library, 1954.

Work, Study, Travel Abroad. New York, N. Y., U. S. National Student Association, 1964.

BOOKLETS AND PAMPHLETS

Bauer, W. W. and Dukelow, Donald A., *What You Should Know About Smoking and Drinking.* Junior Guidance Series, Science Research Associates, Inc., 1955. Chicago, Ill.

Colleges With Room for Students. The Kiplinger Washington Editors, 1963. Washington, D. C.

Exciting Student Tours Abroad. U. S. National Student Association, 1964. New York, N. Y.

Facing Facts About College Admissions. The Prudential Insurance Company of America, 1962. Revised Fall 1962, Spring 1964. Newark, N. J.

Facing Facts About College Costs. The Prudential Insurance Company of America, 1960. Revised 1962, 1964. Newark, N. J.

Facing Facts About the Two-year College. The Prudential Insurance Company of America, 1963. Reprinted 1964. Newark, N. J.

Feingold, S. Norman and List, Harold, *Finding Part-time Jobs.* Science Research Associates, 1962. Chicago, Ill.

Future . . . Jobs for High School Girls. The Women's Bureau, U. S. Department of Labor, 1959. Washington, D. C.

How About College? American School Counselor Association, Division of the American Personnel and Guidance Association, Feb. 1962. Washington, D. C.

How About College Financing? American Personnel and Guidance Association, 1960. Revised 1964. Washington, D. C.

How to Visit Colleges. National Vocational Guidance Association, 1960. Washington, D. C.

If You'd Like to Study Abroad. Guidance Series Booklets, Science Research Associates, Inc., 1963. Chicago, Ill.

Job Horizons for College Women in the 1960's. The Women's Bureau, U. S. Department of Labor, 1965. Washington, D. C.

Margolius, Sidney, *How to Pay for Your Child's College Education.* Public Affairs Pamphlet, 1963. New York, N. Y.

Smith, T. V., *Building Your Philosophy of Life.* Guidance Series Booklets, Science Research Associates, 1953. Chicago, Ill.

Student Travel Abroad. U. S. National Student Association, 1964. New York, N. Y.

Sulkin, Sidney, *Planning for College Costs.* New York Life Insurance Company, 1963. New York, N. Y.

Van Riper, C. *You Can Talk Better.* Junior Guidance Series, Science Research Associates, Inc., 1953. Chicago, Ill.

Zapoleon, Marguerite W., *Girls and Their Futures.* Science Research Associates, 1962. Chicago, Ill.

REFERENCE BOOKS AT YOUR LOCAL LIBRARY

COLLEGE INFORMATION

American Junior Colleges. American Council on Education, Washington, D. C., 1963.

Brownstein, Samuel C., Weiner, Mitchell & Kaplan, Stanley, *You Can Win a Scholarship.* Woodbury, N. Y., Barron's Educational Series, Inc., 1956.

Eskow, Seymour, *Barron's Guide to the Two-Year College.* Woodbury, N. Y., Barron's Educational Series, Inc., 1960.

Feingold, S. Norman, *Scholarships, Fellowships and Loans.* Cambridge, Massachusetts, Bellman Publishing Co., 1955.

Fine, Benjamin, *Fine's American College Counselor and Guide.* Englewood Cliffs, N. J., Prentice-Hall, Inc., 1958-59.

Hawes, Gene R., *The New American Guide to Colleges.* New York, N. Y., New American Library, 1959.

Junior Colleges and Specialized Schools and Colleges. Porter Sargent, Boston, Massachusetts, 1959.

Junior College Directory. American Association of Junior Colleges, Washington, D. C., 1963.

Lovejoy, Clarence E., *Lovejoy's College Guide.* New York, N. Y., Simon and Schuster, 1961.

Lovejoy, Clarence E. & Jones, Theodore S., *Lovejoy-Jones College Scholarship Guide.* New York, N. Y., Simon and Schuster, Inc., 1957.

Thornton, James W., Jr., *The Community Junior College.* New York and London, John Wiley & Sons, Inc., 1960.

VOCATIONAL TRAINING INFORMATION

Cohen, Nathan M., *Vocational Training Directory of the United States.* Washington, D.C., N. M. Cohen, 1958.

Lovejoy, Clarence E., *Lovejoy's Vocational School Guide.* New York, N. Y., Simon and Schuster, 1963.

Where to Find Vocational Training in New York City. New York, N. Y., Vocational Advisory Service, 1964.

Sources for Further Information

The following are suggested sources and addresses from which to obtain more detailed information on specific subjects covered in this book. Some of this source material will be in school and public libraries. Other material can be obtained by writing to the addresses given.

CAREERS IN MEDICINE AND HEALTH

> American College of Hospital Administrators
> 840 North Lake Shore Drive
> Chicago, Illinois 60611

> American Dental Association
> 222 East Superior Street
> Chicago, Illinois 60611

> American Hospital Association
> 840 North Lake Shore Drive
> Chicago, Illinois 60611

> American Medical Association
> 535 North Dearborn Street
> Chicago, Illinois 60610

> American Occupational Therapy Association
> 250 W. 57th Street
> New York, N. Y. 10019

> American Physical Therapy Association
> 1790 Broadway
> New York, N. Y. 10019

> American Veterinary Medical Association
> 600 S. Michigan Avenue
> Chicago, Illinois 60605

National Advisory Commission on Careers in Pharmacy
2215 Constitution Avenue, N. W.
Washington, D. C. 20036

National League for Nursing
Committee on Careers
10 Columbus Circle
New York, N. Y. 10019

The Intersociety Committee on Pathology Information
1785 Massachusetts Avenue, N. W.
Washington, D. C. 20036

The Registry of Medical Technologists
P.O. Box 2544
Muncie, Indiana, 47302

SUMMER EMPLOYMENT OPPORTUNITIES

The Advancement and Placement Institute
169 N. Ninth Street
Brooklyn, N. Y. 11211
"Annual Summer Opportunities for Teenagers"

Barron's Educational Series, Inc.
113 Crossways Park Drive
Woodbury, N. Y. 11797
"Barron's Teen-age Summer Guide"

National Directory Service
Box 32065
Cincinnati, Ohio 45232
"Summer Employment Directory of the United States"

National Federation of Settlements & Neighborhood Centers
232 Madison Avenue
New York, N. Y. 10016
Annual Summer Service Bulletin
"Choose Your Summer Job Now"

U. S. Civil Service Commission
Washington, D. C. 20415
"Summer Employment in Federal Agencies"

TRAVEL AND STUDY ABROAD

American Field Service
313 E. 43rd Street
New York, N. Y. 10017

American Friends Service Committee
160 N. 15th Street
Philadelphia, Pa. 19102

American Youth Hostels
14 W. Eighth Street
New York, N. Y. 10011

Commission on Youth Service Projects
Room 753
475 Riverside Drive
New York, N. Y. 10027

Experiment in International Living
Putney, Vermont 05346

International Christian Youth Exchange
777 United Nations Plaza
New York, N. Y. 10017

National Association of Student Councils
1201 Sixteenth Streeet, N.W.
Washington, D. C. 20036

U. S. National Student Association
265 Madison Avenue
New York, N. Y. 10016

Author's Bibliography

Cox, Claire, *The Upbeat Generation.* Englewood Cliffs, N. J., Prentice-Hall, Inc., 1962.

Gottlieb, David, and Ramsey, Charles, *The American Adolescent.* Homewood, Ill., The Dorsey Press, 1964.

Remmers, H. H., and Radler, D. H., *The American Teenager.* Indianapolis, Ind., The Bobbs-Merrill Co., Inc., 1957.

Schreiber, Daniel, *Guidance and The School Dropout.* Washington, D. C., National Education Association and American Personnel and Guidance Association, 1964.

Splaver, Sarah, *Your Career If You're Not Going to College.* New York, N. Y., Julian Messner, Inc., 1963.

Venn, Grant, *Man, Education, and Work.* Washington, D. C., American Council on Education, 1964.

A Guide to Child-Labor Provisions of the Fair Labor Standards Act. United States Department of Labor, Washington, D. C., 1962.

Havighurst, R. J., and Diamond, Esther E., *Should You Go to College?* Guidance Series Booklets, Science Research Associates, Inc., Chicago, Ill., 1961.

How to Plan Economic Understanding Projects. Education Department, Chamber of Commerce of the United States, Washington, D. C., 1963.

Some Facts for Young Workers About Work and Labor Laws, Bulletin 208, U. S. Department of Labor, 1959.

Spiegler, Charles, and Hamburger, Martin, *If You're Not Going to College.* Science Research Associates, Chicago, Ill., 1959.

Stoops, Emery, and Rosenheim, Lucile, *Planning Your Job Future.* Junior Guidance Series, Science Research Associates, Inc., Chicago, Ill., 1953.

You, Your Job & Your Future. Kiplinger Washington Editors, Inc., Washington, D. C., 1964.

A Study of the Youth Market. Scholastic Magazines, Inc., New York, N. Y., June 1962.

Automation: Nationwide Studies in the United States. Office of Productivity and Technological Developments, Bureau of Labor Statistics, U. S. Department of Labor, 1964. Washington, D. C.

Career Development of Scientists, An Overlapping Longitudinal Study. Graduate School of Education, Harvard University, Cambridge, Mass., 1963.

Follow-Up Study 1962 Graduates of Trade and Industrial Programs in Public Vocational and Technical High Schools, North Atlantic Region, Trade and Industrial Education Branch, United States Office of Education. Printed at Rutgers, The State University, New Brunswick, N. J., 1962.

Hamel, Harvey R., "Employment of School Age Youth, October 1963. *Monthly Labor Review,* Preprint No. 2441, United States Department of Labor, Bureau of Labor Statistics, Washington, D. C., July 1964.

Job Changing and Manpower Training. United States Department of Labor, Manpower Administration, Washington, D. C., June 1964.

Modern Memos. The Modern Talking Picture Service, New York, N. Y. October 1964.

Project Able: An Appraisal. The University of the State of New York. The State Education Department, Division of Research, Albany, N. Y., 1964.

STEP-School to Employment Program, Second Annual Report. The University of the State of New York, The State Education Department, Bureau of Guidance, 1962-1963.

Verrella, Vera C., "Employment of High School Graduates and Dropouts in 1963," *Monthly Labor Review,* Reprint No. 2439, United States Department of Labor, Bureau of Labor Statistics, Washington, D. C., May 1964.

Vocational Education in the Pittsburgh Public Schools. The Pittsburgh Board of Public Education, 1963.

Young Workers: Their Special Training Needs. U. S. Department of Labor, Manpower Administration, Washington, D. C., May 1963.

Youth and Work in New York City. The Taconic Foundation, Inc., New York, N. Y., 1962.

"Planning Your Career For A Changing World." (8 articles in a special issue) *Senior Scholastic,* New York, N. Y., (November 11, 1964).

"Self-Appraisal Appraised—A Letter To Teenagers," *Youth Magazine,* Philadelphia, Pa., (February 3, 1963).

"You and Your Values," *Teen Times Magazine for The Future Homemakers of America,* Washington, D. C., (February-March 1964).

The Author

"Opportunities Unlimited" is not only the name of the job counseling column that Roberta Roesch writes for King Features Syndicate, it also reflects her personal belief.

Mrs. Roesch, a resident of Westwood, New Jersey, has found time to be a writer, teacher, lecturer and editor in addition to being a homemaker and guiding three children of her own. As the author of articles for such magazines as *Parents, American Home, Everywoman's, Better Homes and Gardens, Today's Woman, Your Life, Journal of Lifetime Living* and others, she has interviewed hundreds of people and has gained a keen understanding of the many things that contribute to an individual's success.